Vimla

The Everyday Indian Woman & Murder Most Foul

Vimla

The Everyday Indian Woman & Murder Most Foul

VISHNUPRIYA SITA

Vitasta

Published by
Renu Kaul Verma
Vitasta Publishing Pvt Ltd
2/15, Ansari Road, Daryaganj
New Delhi - 110 002
info@vitastapublishing.com

ISBN 978-93-86473-70-7

First Edition 2021
MRP ₹495

Editorial team: Papri Sri Raman, Mathew Philip, Saraswathi Siva and Aman Ujjwal
Cover and layout: Somesh Kumar Mishra
Printer: Chaman Enterprises, New Delhi

CONTENT

PUBLISHER'S NOTE

Vimla Tyagi's story is that of a good daughter, obedient wife and conscientious mother – the even tenure of whose life is suddenly turned upside down by the country's disruptive economics and politics.

The 1990s was one of the century's most turbulent decades for India. The heady economic reforms had begun under a Rajiv Gandhi-led government, but the country was sitting on a political seesaw. The Indian rupee plunged from 25:1 to 45:1 compared to the USD and inflation swung between 11 to 14 per cent. Market prices of crops like sugar, rice and wheat began to come under the scanner of Commission for Agricultural Costs and Pricing even as big scams like the securities scam, several farm and fodder scams played havoc with the markets and corruption was rampant. The Agriculture Ministry under Balram Jakhar was nowhere near providing competent administration, the ruling party's internal politics just as vicious as its opponents'. Separatist threats from groups like the LTTE, Khalistanis, the Hizbul in J&K, and the armed insurgents of the north-east all besieged the PV Narasimha Rao government. In this setting, when a popular bureaucrat is gunned down in broad daylight and nobody knows why, one is likely to think, this can happen to anyone like you and me. This is why Vitasta brings you the story of *Vimla: The Everyday Indian Woman & Murder Most Foul.*

PROLOGUE

I

1992
The Shadow under the Lamp

For the past two weeks, D/49, Bharti Nagar was seeing a constant flurry of activities. Guests moving in and out, relatives and neighbours coming in to congratulate and contribute to the celebratory arrangements and decorations, and a wide smile etched permanently on every member of the Tyagi family who lived there.

And why not? For when it's your daughter, your only daughter getting married, the preparations for the wedding are not really half-measured. Especially not so when the bride's father is the Chairman of the Commission for Agricultural Costs and Pricing. As an Indian bureaucrat, Devendra Singh Tyagi had risen to the top and was one of the highest-ranking officials in the bureaucracy. His name commanded as much respect in the government and academic circles as he was loved and revered by his friends and family; for ask anyone about Tyagiji and you would be hard-pressed to find someone who would criticise him for either his work or his person. But try praising the man himself, and he would shake it off with a laugh and an air of humility that would only make you think of him in an even higher light.

Devendra Tyagi lived in Bharti Nagar with his wife Vimla, and their three children: Prerna, Prashant and Praveen.

Prerna, the eldest of the three, had applied for a doctorate course in the United States for which she had been selected. Her visa and tickets were ready, and so she was to fly off to another country and start a new life with her soon-to-be-husband after getting married. Everything was in place and the preparations for her final *bidai* were already done; her bags had been packed, clothes, utensils and everything else an Indian family takes with it when shifting to another country already arranged to be shipped ahead of her. The wait was only for the day of her marriage, which, for the bride it seemed couldn't come any slower while for the parents it felt racing by.

On the night before the wedding, the bride's beaming and proud parents had hosted a party at their house for friends and family to celebrate the big sendoff the next day. The entire day had been a joyous occasion for it was the day of Prerna's

mehendi, the Hindu ritual of applying Henna to the bride's hand, making beautiful and intricate designs. For the night's party, their house in Bharti Nagar was decorated to look every bit as beautiful as the bride herself. The who's who of the Indian government were all present, as were the Tyagi family's close friends and relatives.

Devendra, with a soft drink in one hand, was standing in the lawn chatting with his friends and colleagues. He had an air of exuberance around him, the kind which only a bride's father can display, and he talked animatedly with everyone who came to greet him.

The bride's mother, Vimla, was inside the house, sitting with her daughter in her room and trying to have an intimate conversation with her, but with so much commotion and guests who kept pouring in, it was almost impossible to have more than two minutes alone with her.

'You know, when I got married to your father, he used to write me letters from Lucknow while I was in Kanpur. We hadn't even seen each other for almost three months after getting married. But those letters, they were the only saving grace for me during those three months for I just couldn't wait to meet him. You are quite lucky in that sense, I must say. Going off to a new country together with your husband, right after getting married. Let alone three months, I am quite sure you two will not stay separated for even three hours', Vimla said

with a playful nudge to her daughter's side.

'Oh, please stop teasing me Ma. You're one to talk. I know all about your three months and the ones following that too', said Prerna, trying to play cool but barely able to hide her smile too.

As they were both talking about their respective husbands, Praveen walked in and ran to his sister's side, eager to join in on the conversation. 'Enough with this mother-daughter duet, what are you two talking about, I too want to know.'

'Don't you have to complete your homework first?' Prerna asked him, picking on her little brother. 'You first need to get out of school to be able to join in on our conversations.'

Vimla chuckled, but then held her son tightly around his waist and pulled him towards her, 'Don't mind your sister, we were just talking about how her life is going to be like now that she is getting married. But what are you doing in here? Why aren't you outside with all the other guests?'

'Well, actually that is why I am here. I came to take you and *di* outside. Let's go, we are all going to dance now. And I know you are not one to miss out on a reason to dance. And today you have two.'

'Two?' Prerna asked curiously.

'Yeah', he replied. 'One, it's her daughter's wedding and two, she's getting rid of you.'

Laughing, hand in hand, the three exited the room and started walking towards the front door of the house. They were rushed by guests from all

sides, none of who could contain their own love and excitement which poured out as generously as the Tyagi family's hospitality. At the entrance they were met by a couple of young relatives, each grabbing the bride and the mother by their hands and pulling them towards the middle of the lawn... they exclaimed, 'You must dance with us!'

The music in the background was playing some of the hit Bollywood numbers of the time... *Jawani Janeman Haseen Dilruba...Mere Naseeb Mein Tu Hai Ki Nahi...Tu Tu Hai Wahi...Yeh Shaam Mastani...* and within no time almost everyone standing started swinging to the tunes of the music. The more enthusiastic relatives started dancing with their hands in the air and legs rising and falling to the beats of the music, a sight not too uncommon for an Indian wedding. Praveen too joined them, and so did Prashant, followed by their other aunts and uncles who had come all the way from their respective villages in Uttar Pradesh. Some of Devendra's bureaucrat friends too joined the dancing cavalry, for the infectious nature of a wedding dance couldn't keep even the best of them quiet and under the hood for too long. As Vimla and Devendra were dancing in the crowd, their eyes met and they both gave each other a nod of satisfied happiness, smiling from ear to ear for how perfect everything had turned out to be so far.

After a while when everyone had had their fill of food and dancing, the crowd started dispersing.

The guests living in the city left one by one to go back to their own houses, ready to come back the next day for the wedding ceremony. Devendra had arranged for rooms in a nearby hotel for all his guests and relatives who had come from outside Delhi, and he and Vimla saw them off with smiles and hugs and sat them in the vehicles he had arranged to take them to the hotel.

Devendra's brothers insisted they stay with him at the house itself, but he said he would be seeing all of them again the next day and so he wanted them to have a good night's sleep at the hotel rooms which would be more comfortable. Once all the guests had left, he told his house staff to clear the lawn and started walking back inside with Vimla.

'Well, everything went down nicely, wouldn't you say?' Devendra asked, looking to his wife.

'Better than we could have hoped for', she said, smiling at him. 'Now we just have tomorrow to worry about.'

'Oh it's going to be as wonderful as it can be. It is our daughter's wedding', he told her.

Vimla had sent a silent thank you prayer to the Almighty recalling suddenly, the disquiet the day had begun with. Everyone in the house had been asleep still. The day before had been exhausting, with all the running around for the finishing touches and guests arriving. Vimla had woken up early, waiting for the silence to speak the first words of the new day, to hear its first faint sound.

As night tiptoed out of the house and the grey of the sky grew lighter, the doorbell had rung. It was Vimla who had answered the bell as all the others had stirred awake, opening the door to find an old, physically challenged Sardar who asked for Doctor Saab.

'Which Doctor Saab', Vimla had enquired. Her physician brother who was visiting was called Doctor Saab; her bureaucrat husband with a PhD was also called a Doctor Saab. 'Londonwale Doctor Saab'. As Vimla had gone into the house to call her brother, the old man had left.

'It will be perfect', Devendra added, more to himself now than to his wife in revery, and, with his arms around her shoulder and whistling to the tune of one of the songs like a fading echo of the evening's celebrations, they both went back inside.

II

Wedding Bells

It was 6:30 am when Devendra's eyes opened on the morning of 10 May. He turned around in bed to look at his wife, but she was not there. Thinking to himself that she must have started preparing for the day, he too got up. He was mentally taking stock of all the things that needed to be done for the day's ceremony; make sure the *mandap* was ready on time, send over a driver to pick the *panditji* up, talk to the caterer once and ensure food would not run short for anyone... and he walked into the dining room where he heard a voice which broke his train of thought.

'Good morning Tyagiji.'

He looked up and saw his sister-in-law smiling at him. She was sitting with her brother, Dr DC Tyagi, both sipping their cups of tea. Prem and Dinesh were Vimla's two older siblings, and Devendra greatly respected them both. He, in fact, had a very deep and personal bond with DC Tyagi, who was a well-reputed surgeon in London and the two, because of their deep academic interests, would often engage in long conversations on various topics, whether on politics, economics, society or even philosophy. He greeted both of them with the trademark smile on his face.

'Good morning Tyagiji. Come, have some tea', said DC Tyagi, pulling out a chair for Devendra.

Sitting down, he called out to Vimla, who he could hear from the kitchen, to get a cup of tea for him too.

'It's funny how time passes by. My little girl is going to get married today!'

'Well that's true. And would you believe it… it's going to be 25 years of our marriage tomorrow as well', said Vimla, entering the room with a cup of tea in her hand and placing it on the table in front of Devendra.

'Yes, I know. These last few days have been so exhausting, I almost forgot about tomorrow', Devendra replied.

'You don't seem to be running out of reasons for grand celebrations these days. What special events have you two planned for tomorrow?' asked Prem, looking at her younger sister.

'Well, you all will be there, obviously, and we'll also have some friends over. I think we're throwing another party tomorrow', Vimla said, turning towards Devendra.

'Yeah, we are. Tomorrow's going to be a cause for double celebration. Prerna's gotten into a very good doctorate programme, so we are going to celebrate that too.'

The conversation then drifted to the day's events, and they went through all the arrangements that had been done or were left to be done. After a while, Vimla went back into the kitchen to make some breakfast. The other occupants of the house too had started emerging from their rooms; Praveen was still upstairs in his room, while Prashant and Prerna walked in and greeted everyone seated at the dining table.

'Good morning Miss soon-to-be-an-occasional-guest-in-the-house. Come, have some breakfast. This is going to be your last meal as the daughter of this house', Prem remarked, knowing full well this would irk Prerna.

'Nothing that I do will stop me from being my parents' daughter. But you're right *Maasi*, it's not always that all of us sit together for a meal. Prashant will also soon get back to his hostel life and I will be thousands of kilometres away. These moments are rare and blessed.'

As they were talking and relishing this time together, the door bell rang. Devendra looked towards the clock that hung opposite to him on the wall; it was 8:15 am.

'Who could it be this early in the morning?' he wondered.

Prashant was getting up to go see who was at the door, but Devendra pulled his chair back and got up first instead.

'You have your tea; I'll go and see who it is. I

anyway also have to instruct the driver on today's duties.'

Walking across the room, Devendra entered the adjoining hallway which led to the front entrance of the house. As he walked towards the door the bell rang again, and he hastened his pace to quickly reach there, slightly irritated that someone had rung the bell twice, who was it who could not wait a few minutes at this hour? He had asked all his relatives to take their time and come a little late as all the functions would start only after lunch, and all his friends too were supposed to come after lunch. And why weren't Sheetal and Fakir, the two peons who were assigned for his household help, there to see who it was at the door? They should have been the ones coming in with the information. Thinking these things to himself, Devendra opened the door.

Standing at the doorway were two turbaned fellows. One of them was slightly short and the other tall. Devendra could make out they were both young Sikhs, no older than 25, and he wondered what they wanted from him.

'Yes?' he enquired.

'Is Tyagiji home?' the shorter of the two boys asked. He was wearing a black turban and a red chequered shirt. The other one was also wearing a shirt along with a black turban. Devendra noticed they both looked slightly nervous.

'Yes, tell me what happened. How can I help you?'

‘We need to talk to you in private. Can you please step outside for a moment?’ the first fellow asked, pointing to a spot a little outside the door.

‘Why, what happened. Whatever you have to say to me, say it here’, Devendra replied, now slightly agitated by this brazen interruption to his peaceful morning. But being of a very humble and kind nature, he did not want to show his irritation at them. Moreover, they looked to him like two young boys who had come a long way to meet him, perhaps to discuss some of their grievances. They could even be farm boys from Punjab, he thought.

‘If it’s not anything important, I suggest you come back at a later date. I’m actually very busy today. You can maybe take an appointment and meet me at my office if there is something you need to discuss with me’, Devendra told them, and was about to turn and go back inside when he saw a strange movement from the corner of his eyes. The other fellow who had stayed quiet all this while suddenly drew something out which was tucked in his trouser, hidden under the shirt. Not having any time to react, the last thing Devendra saw was the barrel of a gun pointed straight at him.

Three quick shots, and then a fourth.

III

Who Did This?

Inside the house, everyone started at the loud noise which seemed to have echoed all around the building. Vimla looked confused, at first thinking someone had let loose some firecrackers. She turned towards her brother and children, unsure. There were some indistinct shouts coming from outside the house.

Prashant and DC Tyagi got up to go see what was going on when Fakir, one of the peons, came running inside, shouting,

'They shot Tyagiji, they shot Tyagiji!'

His entire body was shaking, and his voice was quivering from the shock of the incident. It took a moment for his words to register among those who were standing in the dining room.

'What, what are you saying?'

'This is absurd. Don't talk nonsense.'

'What do you mean they shot Tyagiji. Who did?'

Rushing to the spot, DC Tyagi was the first to step outside the door. He was aghast at what he saw.

Devendra lying at the entrance in a pool of his own blood. A deep gash was visible on his forehead, from which blood was still gushing out. He immediately rushed to pick up his body and lift his head, trying to reduce the loss of blood. He checked his pulse and shouted at Prashant to call an ambulance. Prashant picked up his phone and dialled the emergency number, called the ambulance, and then rushed outside.

Meanwhile, Vimla also arrived at the entrance, and upon seeing her husband's body lying motionless, with blood streaming all across the floor, she cried out, 'Bhai saab!' She ran towards his side, but her elder brother asked her to not crowd the area and stand back a little. She saw the thick flow of blood that seemed to not stop, and unable to take what was happening, she slumped down and fell to the ground. Prem immediately rushed to her side to help her back on her feet, but Vimla's strengths seemed to have given up on her.

After calling for the ambulance Prahant turned on the househelps. 'Who did this? Who shot him? Where were you? Why weren't you here?' he started firing a stream of questions at Sheetal Prasad and Fakir Chand, who were both too much in shock to immediately give any coherent answer.

Inside, Prerna just stood there at the corner of the room, her mouth cupped in her hands and a look of utter shock and disbelief in her eyes. Praveen was in his room when he heard the gunshot. From his

window, he saw two turbaned guys sitting on a Bajaj scooter heading out of the house in quite some hurry. He noticed Sheetal shouting and running after them, but then the guy sitting behind on the scooter pointed something at him and he dove right into the adjacent hedge headfirst, covering his head with his hands and laying flat on the ground. Confused and unsure, Praveen too rushed down to see what was going on. As soon as he stepped down the last stairs and approached the front door, Prerna saw him and immediately hugged him, breaking down into loud tears.

He saw his mother lying on the ground, shaken to the core but visibly unharmed, with his aunt sitting next to her, tears rolling down her cheeks too. Outside he could hear Prashant talking loudly to someone who he could not see. He then saw the blood, which was all over the floor, a stream of which had trickled to almost reach where he was standing near the stairs. His eyes followed the stream, slowly towards what was lying at the entrance, dreading to see confirmation of what he feared was the worst. And there he saw it, his father, lying there. Just lying. No movement. Blood smeared across his face; his shirt soaked in all red. He saw the look on his uncle's face who was holding his father's hand by the wrist: he hadn't seen a face as white and horrified as his ever before. He clenched his fist as his grip around his sister tightened... He knew that look on his uncle's face meant only one thing.

VIMLA, A GIRL CHILD

ON A RELATIVELY cold night in October of 1947, while all of India was still jubilant in its triumph over British rule, there was another cause for celebration and happiness in a small house in Kanpur. Ramesh Chandra Shastri was sitting in an armchair in the adjoining hall outside his room with his arms folded and his eyes fixed straight ahead at the door that led to his room. He was very anxious and nervous but maintained a stoic expression that did not give away what he was feeling inside. He must have been sitting there for what felt like at least an hour to him, when the door to his room opened with a small creak, and out came an elderly woman who looked at him and said, with a weak smile, 'Congratulations Shastriji, it's a girl.'

Shastri nodded his acknowledgment to the elderly midwife, and when she indicated to him that he could come inside, he followed her into the room to welcome into the world his ninth child.

He saw his wife, Rani, lying on their bed with her back propped up a little with the help of two pillows. She seemed tired and pale, but otherwise healthy. She looked at him as he entered and gave him a smile, which he returned, and then strode across the length of the room to sit by her side on the bed. They both waited as the elderly midwife, along with her assistant who was a woman in her 30s, stood on the opposite side of the bed where Shastri sat and tended to the newborn, who was crying continuously since the time he had stepped into the room. The midwife then wrapped her up in a clean towel and placed the crying baby on her mother's lap.

Shastri looked at his child, his expression still not giving away what he was feeling, and then turned to his wife and said,

'We'll call her Vimla.'

His wife nodded her agreement and bent down low to give her newborn baby a kiss on the cheek.

Shastri could see Vimla's face was flushed with all the crying, which he took to be a good sign. His wife was holding the newborn close to her bosom and singing a soft lullaby, and over their baby's crying, they both looked at each other in silent acknowledgement of what they knew was going to be a long and crucial night. It was important that the baby pulled through the night since having babies in winters always posed an extra challenge, and even then, they knew they had to make extra

efforts to take care of her well-being to ensure a healthy upbringing.

At the time, India had a very poor healthcare infrastructure and was also reeling under the onslaught of many deadly diseases. The average life expectancy of an Indian was very low, just over 30 years, and India fared poorly in infant mortality rate too.

Shastri, of course, knew all this, and not just because he was a well-read scholar and a teacher in a school in Kanpur, but because he and his wife had faced the loss of two children at a young age due to lack of access to proper healthcare services. They lost their second child, Prabha, at the age of 10 when she had contracted a viral flu and never recovered from it. This was three years before Vimla's birth. They had lost another daughter to pneumonia when she was only a year old, shortly before having conceived Vimla. And because Shastri was such a well-read scholar, and himself in very good physical shape, he took it as his personal responsibility to ensure no mortal harm befell any of their children.

VIMLA, THE LITTLE ONE

VIMLA WAS NOW seven years old.

She had, so far, been a healthy and spirited child. In the seven years since her birth, Ramesh Chandra and Rani had another child, a son, who they named Rakesh, and suffered the loss of yet another child, their second son Rajesh who died at the age of nine. Vimla was only two-and-a-half years old then. Vimla's eldest sister, Prem, who was the first born in the house, got married a year after Vimla's birth. She was 16 years old at the time of her marriage, the same age her mother had been when she got married to Shastri.

Vimla's father, Ramesh Chandra Shastri, had a very interesting upbringing. He was not into studies much, and was put into a *gurukul* at a young age. During his years in the gurukul the values of discipline were instilled in him and he had a very strict upbringing. He also got into *pehelwaani* or wrestling while in the gurukul, and after passing his class 10th exam, he took up wrestling as a serious profession. His training and diet were fixed as according to a professional wrestler's, and he took part in exhibition matches and earned money through them.

Interestingly enough, it was during one such match in Lahore which had gathered quite a crowd and was even attended by members of the royal family of the province, that Shastri was offered Rani's hand. Among the enthusiastic crowd was Mahesh, Rani's elder brother, who saw Shastri wrestle and was impressed by his appearance, physicality and strength. After the match was over, he walked up to him and gave him a 1 rupee coin as a token of his appreciation. Soon after, he also gave him his sister's hand in marriage, which Shastri accepted.

Ramesh Chandra was 32 at the time, and in between the fifteen years of his professional wrestling, he had managed to complete his 12th and BA. He had told his father he didn't want to get married and was going to live as a *brahmachari* for the rest of his life. But when Rani's proposal came to him, he accepted and they got married and started a new life together, leaving behind his earlier profession of wrestling.

After the marriage, Shastri and Rani came to Kanpur and bought a house there with the money he had saved up through wrestling. His decision to move to Kanpur was based on the city's proximity

to good schools and colleges. He always regarded education as the most important quality a person should have, and himself got admitted into a master's programme. After doing an MA in English, he also went ahead and got a PhD in Sanskrit. Thereafter, he became a teacher in a school in Kanpur where he taught the English language. He also authored several books, of which some became course books for BA courses in colleges in UP. Through hard work and dedication, he now commanded the well-earned respect of a scholar and an academician in the society they lived in.

So naturally, he expected his children to follow his lead and make education the first focus of their lives. Dinesh Chandra Tyagi, born after Prem and Prabha (who died at the age of 10), was his first son and he wanted him to become a doctor. After Dinesh, they had another daughter, Indu. Then they had two sons, Rajesh (who passed away aged nine) and Umesh. They then had three daughters in quick succession, Manju, Kamla (who died in infancy) and Vimla, who was the youngest of all daughters. Their tenth child was a son, who they named Rakesh.

Vimla's eldest brother, Dinesh, had just completed his schooling and had his medical entrance examinations coming up. So, you could see him cooped up in his room studying for it at all hours of the day. His younger brother Umesh, even though he was still in school, too was similarly focused towards his studies and would try and

emulate the two older male members of the family – his elder brother and his father. Indu and Manju were in school as well, while Rakesh was too young to yet have started his formal education.

Dinesh would sometimes sit by his youngest brother's side and try and teach him the alphabets. Prem, meanwhile had two small children of her own, and she now lived at her in-laws' house in Lucknow. But she kept visiting her parents' house in Kanpur once every couple of months, and on those occasions, Vimla would be very happy as she could play with her young niece and nephew.

Vimla was just two years old when Prem had been married, and her two children were Vimla's playmates, her nephew just four years younger. Vimla's home was their home all their lives, and it was Vimla's father who supported their education and looked after Prem and her family. Prem, as Shastri's daughter, had education in her blood. She was just a school-girl when she had got married and had five pregnancies. Yet she continued her studies, finishing school, and then acquiring BA and MA degrees, encouraged by her father, while her husband barely managed to scrape through his classes and was just educated enough to get a job. Throughout her growing up years, Vimla found her parents so involved with their eldest daughter's well-being that the younger girls in the family had a difficult time convincing their father of the need to pursue their own interests.

VIMLA, BACK FROM DEATH'S DOOR

VIMLA WAS USED to being the pampered child in the house. She was the youngest daughter, and her elder siblings were so much more older than her, it was almost like having surrogate fathers and mothers. Yet, in reality, no one actually paid them exclusive attention, so Vimla enjoyed more freedom which, combined with her love of the outdoors, play or just to roam around, gave her a world of her own. This, naturally, would often mean trouble for her when she got back home. This was because her father was very strict and would not hear any of her nonsense, forcing her to instead stay in the house and study.

It was after one such excursion that on her way back home, she started feeling quite unwell. Vimla, in fact, had not been feeling at her full strength for a couple of days now, but she brushed it off as a passing thing. However, one day when she came back home from school, she had a very bad headache and so a little while after lunch she went out for a walk, thinking some fresh air would do her good. But now as she was walking back home, her head was throbbing as bad as ever while she was also dreading running into her father, which she knew would spell trouble for her.

It was around five in the evening, and she thought her father might have gone out for his usual evening-time stroll. But she still did not want to take any chances, and so instead she skirted around the house and got in through the back door which entered into the kitchen. She slipped out of the kitchen as quietly as possible and headed straight for her room. She paused for a moment outside her parents' room to check if her father was inside, for his armchair in the adjoining hall was empty, but saw through the gap between the door and the doorway that it was just her mother in the room who was taking a nap. She then tip-toed her way into her room, which she shared with Indu and Manju, and got into her bed without even changing or taking notice of who else was there in the room.

'What's the matter?' asked Indu, who was in the room at the time, reading up on a book to prepare for next day's lessons. Studying was all anyone in Vimla's house seemed to do.

'Nothing', came back Vimla's muffled reply, who already had her head buried in the pillow.

'Where had you been off to? You know papa was looking for you. You better have a book in your

hand in case he comes back into the room, looking for you.'

But Vimla did not reply. The long walk and the fresh air did not have the intended effect on the headache she had hoped for. She still felt as if her head was going to split in half, and to add to her woes, she was also now feeling extremely tired and exhausted.

Vimla had already fallen asleep when Shastri came back from his stroll at around 6 in the evening. After sitting down for a cup of tea, which Rani had placed in front of him when he came and sat in his armchair, he went into Vimla's room looking for her. He expected to see her studying, like her sisters Indu and Manju, but instead she was fast asleep. If there was one thing Ramesh Shastri hated, it was the sight of any of his children not optimising their daily routine to find more time to study. Evening time was study time; he thought he had well established this rule in his house. But to come home and find Vimla sleeping instead of doing her homework or preparing for next day's lessons seemed plain ridiculous to him.

'Vimla!' he called out from the door. But she did not respond.

'Vimla!' he called out to her again, his voice slightly more raised this time. She stirred on her bed, mumbled something incoherent in her sleep, but did not wake up. Shastri then walked up to her and reached out for her arm to wake her up. But as soon as he grabbed her arm, he muttered, looking

worried, 'Oh no, her body is very hot. She seems to have fever.'

Turning to his other two daughters in the room, he asked, 'Did she tell you where she had been off to? And when did she come back?'

'No papa, she just came home around 5 and went straight off to sleep. She said something about having a headache in the afternoon, which is why we thought not to disturb her', replied Indu, trying to sound casual.

'Well, she is burning with fever', he said. 'Go tell your mother to bring some cold water and a piece of cloth.'

He then turned to look at Vimla, who had opened her eyes slightly to see what was happening around her. When she saw her father sitting on her bed by her side, she thought he was here to punish her for her earlier misconduct. She wanted to say sorry and apologise for going out yet again without telling him, but too weak to reply or even react to his presence, she just lay there and looked at him appealingly, hoping her eyes would carry the message her tongue failed to deliver.

Shastri perhaps caught on to what she was trying to say, and giving her a comforting smile he said, 'You don't worry about anything *munni,* just lie down and take rest'.

Vimla could not tell from the look on his face, but the father's mind was already taking him to sad and disturbing places. He was thinking about all

his children who had fallen ill just like her, but were never able to make it alive from these illnesses. He thought of Prabha, and how he and Rani had felt when they cremated her and put down her ashes in the Ganga river, watching what remained of their daughter leave their side forever. That was the first time they had faced the loss of their own child. He had hoped to never experience the pain of losing a child again. But life is as ugly and unforgiving as it is beautiful. And Shastri had realised the hard way that the shock of having already lost a child had not prepared him to see the lifeless faces of his other two children when their time came as well. And he knew, it definitely hadn't prepared him to see his youngest daughter bid goodbye from this world too.

While in his mind's eye he could see these dreadful memories being played back to him, at the same time he was looking at Vimla lying on her bed, and he could not help but imagine seeing her take the same path as her brother and two sisters. He thought he would be sick, and forcing himself to think otherwise, he went out of the room to get a thermometer.

Rani, meanwhile, had walked into the room with a look of concern on her face and a bowl of water in her hands. She sat beside her daughter and placed her hand on her forehead, letting out an audible gasp. 'My god munni, for how long have you been feeling unwell?'

'I don't know, a couple days maybe. But I had a very bad headache today when I was in school', Vimla replied back. However, she could see her mother looked extremely worried and knew she would somehow blame herself for not knowing sooner that her daughter was sick. So, she added with a smile, 'But it's nothing. I will be fine by tomorrow morning you see. I'm probably just a little exhausted from all the activities we had in school today.'

Rani didn't say anything, but instead started wiping Vimla's forehead and arms with the wet cloth she had brought with her in the bowl. She first soaked the cloth in the water and then wrung it to semi-wet, and then softly dabbed at the edges of Vimla's eyes, her forehead, and then her arms. She continued with this exercise without saying anything, hoping maybe the silence in the room would somehow make the prayers in her head louder for the gods to hear and they would bring her daughter back to full health.

As she continued with her efforts to bring Vimla's body temperature down a little, Shastri walked back into the room with a thermometer in his hand. He sat beside his daughter and asked her to open her mouth and roll her tongue. He then gently placed the thermometer under her tongue and then waited. He could see the mercury rising steadily, shining morbidly in the light of the bulb hanging above them, and with it his panic, which

he was trying hard to keep at bay, rising too. After a couple of minutes, he took the thermometer out from Vimla's mouth, and then held it over his head at an angle so that he could accurately make out what the reading was.

'101 degrees', he muttered slowly, almost under his breath. He then turned to his wife and said, 'You wait here by her side and keep applying wet cloth to her forehead. I'll go and see if I can get a doctor to come and check on her'. With that, he turned around and left in a hurry.

It must have been an hour since Shastri had left when they heard a knock on the door. Vimla had fallen asleep again, and Rani had now placed the semi-wet cloth over Vimla's eyes and forehead, removing it, dipping it in water and placing it back on her once every ten minutes or so. But neither the cold water nor Rani's incessant prayers seemed to have had any effect on Vimla's fever. Indu and Manju were now sitting by their sister's side, and Umesh too had come in to see how she was doing. When the knocker struck the door, Rani said to Umesh, 'It must be your father back with the doctor. Go open the door for them.'

Umesh went outside to open the door, and a minute later Shastri entered the room briskly followed by a bespectacled man who walked in with a briefcase in his hand, with Umesh tailing behind them both. The doctor was led to Vimla's bed by Shastri, who motioned to Indu and Manju

to clear the bedside. Umesh pulled a chair from the corner of the room and placed it near Vimla's head on the bedside so that the doctor could sit there. He was briefly introduced to Rani by Shastri, and then asked to examine Vimla.

The doctor took the chair and drew it closer to Vimla so that he could have a better look at her. She was still sleeping. He placed his hand on her shoulder, and gently nudged her so that she would wake up. After another nudge, Vimla woke up.

She opened her eyes just a fraction and saw the outline of someone's face looming over her head, bent low. She blinked once, and then again. The outline became sharper and the face came slowly into view; it was not a face she recognised. She could see the man, whoever it was, was smiling at her. She looked to the man's left, and saw her father standing there, his arms folded as usual. A little behind the man, to his right, she saw her mother was there too. She then turned her eyes back towards the man sitting beside her, who still wore a warm, gentle smile on his face.

'Hello Vimla, my name is Rahul Singh', the man said.

'Hi', Vimla replied softly.

'I am a doctor and I have come to check on your health. I'm going to ask you to do a few simple tasks for me, ok?' he said kindly.

'Okay.'

'Open your mouth and stick out your tongue.'

She did as she was told. The doctor then held a small flashlight and peered into her mouth.

'Ok, now say "aaaaaaa."'

'Aaaaaaaaa', Vimla repeated after him.

'Good girl. Now I want you to keep this under your tongue for a minute', he said and pulled out a thermometer from inside his briefcase. He shook the thermometer vigorously and then placed it in her mouth. After a minute, he took it out and observed the reading and then wiped its end with his handkerchief and put it back inside his case without saying anything. He then took out a stethoscope from inside the briefcase, put on the earpieces and started probing her chest and stomach with the disc end. After a couple minutes of probing and listening he returned the stethoscope from where he had taken it, again without uttering a word. He then closed the briefcase and placed it on the floor beside his chair.

'Okay Vimla, since when have you been feeling unwell?'

'Well I started having this terrible headache in school today. But I have been feeling a little unwell for the past two or three days now', said Vimla, in a slow monotone.

'Headache, huh? Do you have body ache as well, legs, back or anywhere else?' the doctor enquired.

'Not too much. But I feel very exhausted', she mumbled back.

'Hmm, ok. Well don't worry. You just need to take some rest. I am giving you some medicines, take them and you'll be up and about in no time!' said the doctor, trying to sound cheerful.

He then pulled his chair back, picked up his briefcase and got up to leave. He jerked his head at Rani to acknowledge his goodbye, and then walked outside with Shastri. The two men walked quietly till they reached the door to the main exit, where Dr Singh turned to Shastri and said, 'It seems to be simple fever, and I have given the medicine for today and tomorrow. That should bring the fever down. But I have my suspicions that she could have typhoid'.

At his last word, a look of shock registered in Shastri's eyes.

'Don't worry, it's just a suspicion', Dr Singh said consolingly. 'In any case, do let me know if the fever persists. And also check her stool, whether it's normal or watery.'

'Okay', Shastri replied back. 'But you're certain there's nothing to worry about and she'll get better?' All his fears were still alive.

'Well… you keep me posted about her health and pray her fever comes down. But if it persists, we'll have to see what is to be done.'

'Okay, I'll let you know. Thank you so much for agreeing to come and see her at this hour.'

And with that, he bid the doctor goodbye and closed the door behind him.

VIMLA ON THE RECOVERY CURVE

THAT NIGHT VIMLA slept with her parents, lying between Rani and Ramesh. Rani had given Vimla rice-starch water meal for dinner, after which Vimla took the medicine and had slept off. Rani had kept the bowl of water on the floor beside the bed, and had continued placing the cloth on Vimla's forehead right through the night.

The next morning, Vimla woke up with a heavy head. Her fever had somewhat reduced as a result of the coupling effect of both the medicine and Rani's constant application of wet cloth. However, even with the reduced fever, Vimla still felt drained of all energy and couldn't even get up to go to the bathroom. She looked at the clock that hung on the wall opposite the bed, and saw that it was ten past nine. Her father and her siblings must surely be in school now, she thought. So, it must be just her mother and her eldest brother Dinesh in the house, since he had completed school and was preparing at home for college entrance examinations. She could hear her mother working in the kitchen, and so she called out to her. Realising her meek voice would perhaps not carry to her, she tried calling her again, a little louder.

There was a noise of a few utensils scraping, and then the next moment, her mother's face appeared in the doorway, peering inside. When she saw her daughter was up, she gave her a huge smile and said, 'Look who's up!'

'How are you feeling now?' Rani added, sounding hopeful.

'I don't know. I still don't feel too good', Vimla said sadly. 'I need to go to the bathroom and I need your help. I don't think I have the strength to do it on my own.'

'Well of course', she said, coming into the room and helping Vimla off the bed.

After assisting Vimla to the washroom, Rani also helped her brush her teeth, and then even gave her a sponge-bath; cleaning her body with wet cloth. She then helped her change into fresh clothes and put her back to bed. She fed her, and then gave her the medicines, after which Vimla, feeling too exhausted to do anything, went back to sleep.

Vimla slept throughout the day, and did not wake up even when her father returned from school in the afternoon. Rani had tried giving her some lunch, but after a few measly bites, Vimla did not feel like eating and went back to sleep. Her fever

too had crept up, and the atmosphere in the house started becoming tense by the minute.

That night, Rani tried force feeding Vimla some rice-starch water meal so that they could give her medicines. Vimla obliged, though with no real energy, and then slept off immediately after taking her medicine.

The following day saw no improvement in Vimla at all. Her fever was at an all-time high. Shastri had checked her temperature with the thermometer in the morning before going to school, and it had showed above 103° Fahrenheit. This was reason to worry, and Shastri had started thinking what the next best course of action would be. There were a couple of government hospitals nearby, but he was aware the treatment there was below par. There was no question of getting Vimla admitted there, as he knew she would surely be better taken care of at home than at those hospitals. He remembered what the doctor had said about maybe having to treat her for typhoid, and decided he would ask him to pay another visit tonight if Vimla's condition did not improve during the day.

And Vimla's condition did not improve, but only deteriorated. She now lay still as a brick on the bed and would get up only to go to the washroom, assisted at all times by Rani. Her loss of appetite was made worse as now she also had diarrhoea, and as a result she was drained of even the little energy that was left in her.

In the evening when Shastri went out to call on the doctor and returned home with Dr Singh, Vimla was in deep sleep. She barely opened her eyes when Dr Singh tried waking her up, and then closed them back again. He did a routine check up of her body temperature, pulse and heartbeat, and then asked Rani how her bowel movements had been. When he learned that she was having loose motions, he nodded gravely and said, 'My suspicions were correct. She seems to have typhoid'.

Taking out a small notepad from the inner pocket of his coat, he wrote out a different set of medicines for Vimla and handed it out to Shastri, adding, 'Also make sure she gets lots of fluids to drink. And while you're at it, get as many fresh fruits as you can for her as well'. With that he got up and proceeded to leave, but not before motioning to Shastri to meet him outside.

Following him outside, Shastri walked up to where Dr Singh was standing in the hall and gave him a quizzical look.

'I didn't want to say it in front of Rani, but Vimla's case is quite serious', Dr Singh said with genuine concern in his voice. 'I just want you to be prepared for any...er...undesirable outcome.'

The lines around Shastri's mouth tightened. He looked gravely at Dr Singh and opened his mouth to say something, but words seemed to have failed him. Dr Singh placed a firm hand on his shoulder and said in a forcefully cheerful voice, 'I'm just trying to alert

you to certain possibilities. Doesn't mean they are going to come true. You give her the medicines and make sure she gets lots of fresh fruits to eat, and I'm sure she will be back on her feet in no time.' Ramesh, still unable to bring himself to say something, simply nodded and bid the doctor goodbye.

The following fortnight went by in frantic anticipation. The doctor's words of caution seemed to have put Shastri into a deep state of resolve, and he did all he could to bring his daughter back to full health. Although they were not particularly poor, Shastri still ran his household on a shoestring budget owing to the fact that he had a dozen or so mouths to feed at home. However, this did not hold him back from providing Vimla with every chance for her to fight off her illness, build her immunity and regain her strength. He would go out every evening and buy fresh fruits for her, and none of the other children were allowed to have from her share of fruits. Along with that, Rani had also prepared ORS at home by adding sugar and salt in water in the appropriate ratio and giving it to Vimla from time to time to help with the diarrhoea. They had placed Vimla on a carefully monitored diet along with giving her the prescribed medicines timely.

Slowly, with constant care and tending, Vimla started recovering. Although there had been a moment of scare when Vimla's body temperature had crept up to 104°F one night, but by the following morning the fever had reduced and Vimla

had started feeling better, thanks in no small part to Rani who had stayed awake the entire night dabbing Vimla with wet cloth to bring down the fever.

It was a slow and continuous process to bring Vimla back to full health, and by the third week, Vimla could get out of the bed and do most of the things herself. Her recovery had put everyone in the house in a good mood, and one could perceive the tense atmosphere that had engulfed the house for the past three weeks evaporate. Vimla had had a close brush with death, and this was not lost on Shastri or Rani who knew only too well how very near they had been to losing another child. They both breathed a sigh of relief when at last they saw their youngest daughter back to her usual self, bustling in and out of the house like they had grown used to seeing her.

But unbeknownst to them all, a nervous anxiety had started overcoming Vimla. She knew, her three weeks off school meant only one thing now that she was back on her feet again; copiously studying what she had missed so far which would undoubtedly cut down on her outdoor wanderings. And there would be no escaping this time, for she was sure she would be kept under her father's nose at all times.

And true to her fears, Shastri's constant vigilance was as severe as any Vimla had ever seen. He had accompanied her to the school on her first day back and met with her teacher, asking him to provide notes

for all the lessons she had missed in the past three weeks. And so, every day from that day onwards, when Vimla got back from school she not only had to finish that day's homework, but also had to keep going back to her missed lessons and copy those notes as well. If at all she thought she could leave some work for the next day, her father was always around to ensure that she toiled without respite. All this work meant that she no longer had time to do any of the things she loved doing; playing, listening to songs or stepping outside for her little excursions, or in other words things her father considered an utter waste of one's time.

But Vimla being Vimla, had soon began finding ways to weave her way around the stringent routine her father had set for her. Moreover, she had now caught up with her lessons which meant no more putting in the extra hours that she earlier had to, and so more time to get back to her old self. This meant that she had once again started spending more time roaming around and in her own dreamy world, with her studying hours coming few and far between her many other interests, one of which had become listening to the radio.

VIMLA, MOVIE MAD

VIMLA LOVED LISTENING to the radio. It was something she was fascinated by since the first time she heard voices and songs coming out of the tiny box as she was crossing the local tea vendor one day who had got the novelty item to attract more customers to his shop. And since there was no such thing as a radio around her house ('What an ingenious way to keep people from working', Shastri had once said about the radio, dismissing the idea of getting one for their home when the topic was brought up), Vimla resorted to lingering at the tea shop which was right around the corner of her house whenever she got the chance; on her way to school, on her way back, during casual strolls, volunteering to accompany Dinesh or Umesh to help get grocery… any excuse to go out of the house which could be found, Vimla would find it.

In the absence of any other fluid medium, radio had become an integral medium of communication across the country through which news of national importance like national security or government schemes were announced, but the main attraction was of course the latest hits of the time being broadcasted on it. Radio in India had become a prime medium for social integration and gatherings, and Vimla a prime consumer of it. She knew if her father found out or caught her in the act, she would get a sound beating for it. But she was hooked to it like a fish to its bait; notwithstanding consequences, both inevitably swimming towards their imminent doom.

For Vimla though, her little packets of joy which were bundled in that small corner near her house seemed to only increase with time. Whether it was fate that was on Vimla's side, or her father had chosen to take a lighter view of things where she was concerned, Vimla somehow never found herself on the wrong end of her father and it continued like this for her for a few years.

Buoyed by this lack of deterrence, Vimla's thirst to explore the many reams of the entertainment industry only increased now that she was a little older. She had heard all about cinemas from her friends in school, some of who had gone to watch movies with their parents. Listening to her friends talk about their experiences left Vimla secretly nursing a jealous spot, and she was dying to get a taste of the *bada parda* for herself. But she knew she would have more luck convincing a lion to have tea

with her than convince her father to take her to the movies, and so resorted to the only option she was left with; her mother.

The following few days she carefully plotted the course to convincing her mother. She would wake up early and assist her mother in the kitchen. She would come back from school and sit down to do her homework first thing after having lunch. She would even stay back in the evening and not go out, instead again helping her mother around the house and, sometimes even sitting down to study for the next day's lessons. The change in her daughter had put Rani in an amusingly surprised mood, exactly what Vimla had been hoping for. And then a few days later, risking her moment when her father was not at home and all her siblings were far from earshot, Vimla went for it.

Having already prepared exactly what she was going to say to her mother, she went through it all over again in her head so that nothing goes wrong. Rani was in her room folding clothes and putting them in the almirah.

'Hey ma, need some help with that?' Vimla crooned, her head popping from behind the doorway. Then, entering the room with weighted anticipation, she began folding the clothes along with her mother before Rani could say anything.

'What has gotten into you these days?' Rani asked with a smile, her voice shrouded in amusement.

'Oh nothing, I just see you doing so much work around the house I thought I should also be lending my hand. So that's what I am doing', Vimla piped.

Rani just pinched her cheek playfully in response, and then both mother and daughter began folding the clothes laid on the bed. After a few minutes, Vimla started humming the tune to a song she had heard on the radio, a tune she had carefully picked and rehearsed beforehand for it was from a film that was being screened at the cinema halls then. She knew it was important to not make the first move and was waiting for Rani to say something, which didn't take long to happen.

'What is that song?' Rani said, turning towards Vimla. 'It's got a nice ring to it.'

'It's from a new movie, *Mother India.* I hear it play on the radio all the time when I go to school', Vimla replied back, going back to her humming.

A few more minutes passed before Vimla, knowing the time was right, said in an airy voice, 'Say mother, you work so hard the entire day… as do I'. Then she added, in a slightly exasperated tone, 'I think we both deserve some break'.

'What kind of a break are you talking about', asked Rani, eyeing her daughter carefully.

Waiting exactly for this moment, Vimla said quickly and in one single breath, 'I-think-we-should-both-go-watch-a-movie-this-Saturday-at-the-cinema-theatre'.

Not prepared for such a reply, it took a second for Rani to register what Vimla had actually suggested. But as soon as she recovered from the initial shock, she was more amused than angry at her daughter's attempt to woo her into doing something she knew her husband would never grant them permission for. So, when she replied, her voice was rather kind, in fact pitiful towards her daughter.

'Aahh, so this explains the last few days of veiling yourself in sainthood. You had left me wondering what has happened to my daughter to suddenly become so obedient and well-behaved.' Then sitting Vimla on the bed, she continued softly, 'You know how papa is like. Even if I want to take you, he won't allow'.

'But ma, I know you can convince him if you want to. Please please, please, I really want to go watch this movie. It's *Mother India* and I've heard it's a really good movie', Vimla cried. 'You are the only person who can make this happen, because you are my mother India!' she added with a sly smile on her face.

'Ha ha ha, I can see how desperate you are. But no, I don't think this is a good idea', Rani said, but lacking just enough conviction to make Vimla rile on further. 'No ma, this is a really good idea. The movie has all the big stars, how can it not be a good idea. Please you talk to papa, and let's go this Saturday'.

Making her eyes as big and wide as possible, Vimla looked at her mother hard and strong, trying

to melt her way into her heart.

'Stop looking at me like that! Ok fine, FINE. If we are to do this, you will listen to everything that I have to say.'

'Of course', said Vimla, without thinking.

'You will complete all your homework *and* prepare for next day's lessons *every day until Saturday*. If your father wants to crosscheck your work, which I am sure he will, you make sure he finds no reason to be unhappy with you. Otherwise you can forget going to the movies', said Rani in a serious tone.

'Ok, I will.'

'Good', Rani said. And then concealing a smile, she added, '*And,* you will continue helping me with household work like you were doing.'

A look of surprise mingled with some shock registered on Vimla's face. She looked at her mother in disbelief, but then said, 'Well ok, I guess that one's on me.'

'But ma, how are you going to ask papa to give permission to take us to the movie?' asked Vimla, a little apprehensive but more curious.

'That is not for you to worry. You just keep yourself on your best behaviour this week and do as I say. Leave the rest to me', replied Rani.

Vimla did not know how her mother had managed to do it, but Rani had somehow taken permission from their father to let her take Vimla, Manju and Indu to the movie on Saturday. Vimla

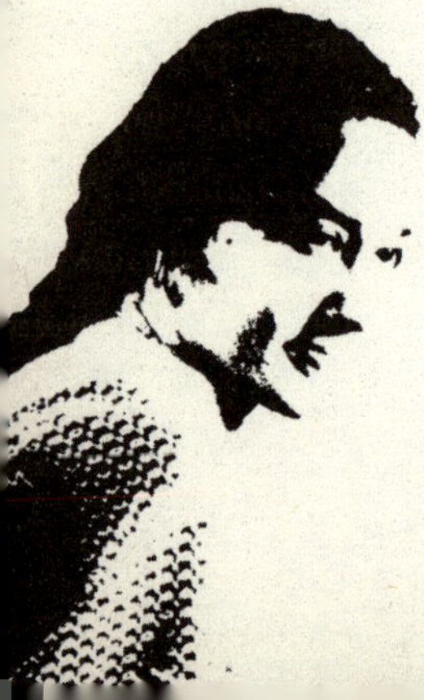

was ecstatic when Rani told her that they were indeed going to go watch *Mother India* at the cinema theatre. 'I can't believe this, I can't believe this!' she kept saying, jumping up and down with uncontained joy.

Although it was only four days till Saturday, for Vimla it seemed as though the fabric of time had been stretched so much that she could fit in entire life cycles in each passing second of the week. But not once did she waver from her promise to her mother, for the thought of finally being able to see what she had only yet heard of from her friends made it easier for her to drudge on with her work.

Every day until Saturday was an anxiety feast for Vimla as she kept thinking something would go wrong, or her father would withdraw his permission, and they would not be able to go watch the movie. But Saturday arrived with as much promises and intent in store as Vimla had been dreaming about for so long. When she woke up in the morning, her heart felt swollen to the size of a balloon and her head dizzy with the many thoughts and imaginations that had run amok in her brain on how she was going to spend the day.

The time it took for her to get out of the bed and get dressed to go for the movies must have been some kind of a world record. She was so happy that even her father afforded a smile when she came out into the living room to greet him and he saw her all dressed up and ready to go.

'I don't think I have ever seen you bathed and ready by 8 am on a Saturday', her father remarked in obvious jest. 'If only you showed such enthusiasm towards your studies as well', he added sternly, as if to compensate for his earlier mirth.

But Vimla was in such a good mood that she would have lapped up anything her father said, and right now she thought he was being rather friendly. Shrugging slightly at her father's remarks, Vimla said, 'I try papa, but every time I concentrate on my books it gives me a headache. What am I....'

'Don't start with that headache nonsense again', Shastri derided, cutting Vimla short. 'Your excuses are just as weak as you are. You should learn from your elder brothers and sisters. See how dedicated they are towards studies.'

Vimla thought it was very unfair that she was being scolded thus, especially when she had worked so hard the previous week. And it was not like she was making excuses, she had actually started getting headaches, every time she tried to concentrate hard on her chapters. The injustice of the situation made Vimla want to say something back to her father, but she knew better and thought best to merely apologise and not make any further arguments lest her father cancel their movie programme.

She mumbled a soft apology and was waiting for her father's rebuke again, but fortunately for her Rani walked in with a cup of tea at that moment and Shastri did not pursue the subject any further. Upon seeing her mother, Vimla's thoughts immediately jumped back to the day that lay ahead of them, and greeting her mother enthusiastically she asked, 'What time will we be leaving ma? We don't want to be late'.

'Calm down *munni,* there is plenty of time before we leave. You go see where your sisters are and call everyone for breakfast', said Rani as she placed the cup in front of her husband.

Humming to herself, Vimla spun around and hopped out of the room, calling out to her sisters and brothers in a sing-song voice. Soon after everyone had gathered, had their breakfast and left for their respective work that day, Vimla came back to the table to sit with her mother as she ate her meal; Rani always had her food alone after everyone in the family had had theirs.

'You are incredible ma! I cannot believe you convinced papa to let us go for the movie', Vimla said, her voice full of excited quiver.

'You know, my friend was telling me that all big superstars are there in *Mother India*. She was saying this is the best Hindi cinema made till date', Vimla told her mother in a very matter-of-fact tone. 'Even the songs in the movie are all amazing and sung by the best singers', she went on.

Vimla kept rattling on everything she had heard about the movie from her friends as Rani was having her breakfast. She kept at her mother's tail talking animatedly about everything that was in store for them as Rani went about finishing all the morning chores, and only stopped when Rani finally went to her room to take a bath and get dressed.

Soon, the three sisters – Indu, Manju and Vimla – led by Rani were out walking, chatting and laughing their way towards the cinema theatre which was located at the centre of the town, some five kilometers from their house. If Vimla's excitement was visible throughout morning, it was nothing compared to how she was feeling as they walked together. She thought her heart, which felt like a balloon in the morning, would burst with elation. The prospect of going out on a Saturday with her mother for a movie was alien to her just a week ago; and here she was now, slowly making her way to realising one of her dreams.

The entire journey from their home to the cinema theatre, Vimla hardly kept her mouth shut, chattering away continuously about what they might experience and what it would be like watching a movie on the big screen. Upon reaching the place, she accompanied her mother to the ticket booth while her two sisters waited nearby. While they were both standing in the queue, Vimla turned to her mother and asked,

'Look at the crowd ma, so many people have come to watch the movie. What if we don't get tickets?'

'Pray that doesn't happen, my child. And if it does, well there's always a next time for everything', replied Rani with a soft smile on her face.

When she saw the worried look still etched upon Vimla's face, Rani bent down to level with her daughter and said, 'Remember how excited you were this entire week to watch this movie? It was because of you and your willingness to watch it in a theatre that we are here. If you truly want something and work hard for it with the purest intent in your heart, you will definitely get it one way or the other. If you don't, understand that it must not be the right time for that thing to happen. But does that mean you should stop working for it, stop nursing that desire in your heart. No. We have great power in our mind and heart to achieve and make true whatever it is we desire the most. And if the time wasn't right then, it will be right later, and when that happens there is *nothing* in the world that will stop you from having what it is you wanted. Always remember that, munni'.

Placing her finger first on Vimla'a chest and then her temple, Rani whispered with a smile, 'It's all about your heart's desire and your mind's willingness to achieve it'

She then got up and proceeded to move forward in the queue, holding Vimla by her hand who was still deep in thought, contemplating the worldly wisdom her mother had just imparted.

It's funny how impressionable some words, some people and some places can be on someone. Their father, Ramesh Shastri was a learned scholar,

an articulate man who regularly advised and gave counsel to his children on what was right and what was wrong, what they should do and what they shouldn't do. Their house was like a synthesis of school and temple, where virtues of education, knowledge and morality were constantly being drilled into its residents. But notwithstanding all those years of teachings her father imparted, it was here, in the middle of a crowded place that a woman lacking in any formal education made one of the most lasting impression on Vimla. She took to heart the lesson her mother gave that day, never forgetting to keep desiring, to keep working for it.

Soon they reached the front of the queue and Vimla, taking charge, said to the guy sitting behind the counter, '*Bhaiya,* give us four tickets to *Mother India*'. Standing on her toes and craning to see from over the top of the counter as she could barely reach its height, Vimla collected the tickets promptly while Rani paid for them. As soon as she had the tickets with her, Vimla ran towards her sisters and held the tickets out proudly for them to see. 'We got it, we got it. Finally, we can now watch a movie at a cinema hall!' exclaimed Vimla as she waved the tickets frantically up and down her sisters' faces.

'Ha, ha, with you standing here and bobbing like a monkey I don't think we need to go inside for entertainment', said Indu. 'But I must say, I am impressed.'

Vimla, who had the widest grin plastered across her face, delightfully grunted acknowledgment of her sister's remarks. They were then joined by Rani who announced to her children, 'The movie starts in 10 minutes. We should go inside and take our seat. C'mon now, follow my lead and everyone hold each other's hand'. And with that, she led the three girls to the front grilled gate, where there seemed to be a struggle going on for getting in.

A lot of the crowd was made up of young men who were trying to force their way into the gate, while two burly men were standing at the entrance doing just enough to allow only legitimate movie goers entry into the hall. Rani squeezed her way forward, trying to push the crowd apart with one hand while holding Vimla's hand firmly with the other as she kept shouting, 'Ladies coming through. Please give way'. The four somehow managed to hustle their way to the front of the crowd where Rani held out the tickets for the security guards to see, who then let them in.

As they walked inside, they found themselves in a corridor with winding stairs on either ends of it. There were three double-doors on the wall across the corridor; one in the middle and two at the far corners of the corridor. Rani led the three in through the one in the middle and on entering, Vimla let out an audible gasp.

'Woah, we can fit in our entire house inside this hall; it's so big!' she exclaimed.

While Vimla stood there gaping at the grandiose of it all, Rani gave the tickets to an usher who stood nearby. He took a look at the tickets and then led the four of them towards the bottom end of the hall. Around 5 rows from the very bottom he stopped, and then pointing his flashlight at four empty seats in the middle of the row he said, 'There you go, those are your seats'.

The four shuffled their way through to their seats and sat down. Vimla, who sat down between Rani and Indu, had her eyes fixed ahead where she could only see a big red curtain in front of her. Vimla sat rigid, not sure what to expect as the hall began filling with the sound of hundreds of feet shuffling around, people chatting while getting into their seats, bursts of laughter erupting from random sections and echoing across the hall, and vendors going up and down the aisles calling out, 'popcorn, cold drinks'. Her already rigid body stiffened even further when the surrounding clamour suddenly gave way to a hushed silence as the red curtain began rising, revealing a white screen. All her efforts, all her trepidations, everything she had worked for this last week had built up to this moment, and as the curtain rose she could feel her hysteria rising along with it, building to a crescendo which ended with a little yelp of excitement as soon as the screen lit with the first signs of motion picture.

Vimla was rooted to her spot from the moment the movie opened with its iconic image of an old

Nargis, to the closing scene where the movie ended exactly where it began. What transpired in between took Vimla along for an emotional and cathartic ride that was as powerful as the movie itself. She was numb from the intensity of everything she was feeling, never knowing that watching a movie could have such a powerful effect on her. She was so moved, so touched, so enamoured by Nargis' portrayal of Radha that words failed to express her feelings, for when after the movie, Rani turned to Vimla and asked, 'So, how did you like it?', she could only look at her mother with welled up eyes and hugged her tightly.

Vimla's demeanour could not have been farther from what it was before the movie began. Where before she was all jittery, restless and talkative, she was now unusually calm and quiet, as if trying to internalise everything that she saw and felt. Lost in thought, she walked behind her mother, unconsciously grabbing the hem of her saree edge, as the four made their way back home.

VIMLA, OF THE DANCING FEET

FOR THE FIRST few months after having watched *Mother India*, Vimla was entirely consumed by it and would only talk about what she liked about the cinema, especially its music. Her love for cinemas and music grew massively over the course of time, but she had to contend with watching movies in the theatre with her mother only once every few months or so.

Vimla had become so infatuated by music that she started accompanying Indu in the after school hours to a music school, where Indu took music lessons. While Indu took her lessons in classical music, Vimla would just sit there and listen to her play instruments and sing. As someone whose mind was mostly restless, surrounding herself in music helped Vimla soothe and calm her senses to a yet undiscovered degree. Here, she would be at peace; the only time she felt her mind and soul in harmony, lost in the musical abyss of her sister's melodies.

Even though Vimla was just a passive participant to her sister's playing music, joining Indu on her lessons gave Vimla a new-found enthusiasm for something to look forward to after school. More so, because school had become a druggery for Vimla who felt completely out of place amidst the books and lessons which she just could not grapple with, try hard as she may. Irony had played its cruellest game with Vimla; for even though her entire family had a very strong educational background and everyone from her father to all her siblings were soaked in the ideals of literary discipline from head to toe, Vimla just could not fit the bill in academia. She couldn't care less about her lessons of the day, and would instead spend most of her time in class gazing out of the window, day-dreaming, humming the tune of the latest songs she had heard on the radio or just chatting away with her classmates. The recess time was her favourite part of going to school as she could go outside and play with her friends; the one thing that brought life and joy to her face when in school.

Her lack of adjustment with classroom studies naturally translated into her exam results where she consistently fared poorly, barely scraping through to progress into the next standard every year. However, her substandard marks or indifference towards books did not deter Vimla from pursuing her other interests. While her older siblings fretted about their marks, how to put in more hours of

study, or what they wanted to do in the future, Vimla would simply not be bothered by any of it. If anything, her siblings' attitudes and their seriousness towards studies amused her. And being the youngest daughter perhaps saved her from the severity of Shastri's ire, usually directed towards those who would not study, for none of the other children in the Shastri household enjoyed as much freedom and liberty to simply while their time away as Vimla did.

For Vimla, however, spending time on things and activities which her father considered unworthy did not feel futile at all. In fact, it was on one such occasion when Vimla had gone with Indu for her music lessons that she discovered a facet to her life which had hitherto been buried deep within her; her love and passion for dance. Vimla had grown fond of dancing and had been nursing a latent desire to learn how to dance since she had watched some of the movies with good dance numbers, especially *Madhumati* in which the ethereal Vyjayanthimala had captured her imagination like never before.

It had been just another day for Vimla who, while listening to Indu's singing, got a little distracted and went outside for a walk. As she was strolling aimlessly around the corridor, she walked by a classroom where she saw a dozen or so girls huddled around an elderly woman listening to her talk to them about something. Wondering what they were up to, Vimla walked closer to the door

and stood by it so she could get a better look at the group.

The elderly woman was making some gestures with her hand, and then pointing to the girl nearest her, she said, 'Your arm movements need to be as fluid and pristine as the clear stream of water running through the valleys of the Himalayas. You have to loosen up your body, and only then can you hope your movements to have the grace and elegance of a good dancer'. She then did a quick turn on the spot and waved her arm around her head in an effortlessly elegant move, demonstrating to the girl what she meant.

The woman's movements caught Vimla's attention faster than a lightning bolt on its way down from the clouds to the earth; she was now rooted to her spot and had eyes and ears only for what the woman was doing.

As the girls followed the woman's lead while she taught them various dance moves, Vimla stood there inconspicuously, following the woman's every step, spin and swoon to the minutest of detail. Time stood still for Vimla as she watched the woman dance, trying to mimic her moves from her spot near the door. She knew not how long she had been there dancing to her heart's own rhythm, and it was only when Indu, who had come searching for her sister, interrupted her that Vimla broke away from her seemingly euphoric trance.

'What are you doing here? I have been looking

for you for the last 15 minutes! You could have at least told me where you were going', Indu said vehemently, grabbing Vimla by her arm.

Indu's admonishments seemed to be coming from a far off distance for Vimla, who was still in effect thinking about the woman inside the room. She mumbled an incoherent apology and then followed Indu back to her music class. But from that day on, Vimla would go and secretly watch the group dance every time she went with Indu, and each day she would come back home and practice the steps she remembered in front of the mirror in her room. This went on for a week until one day, as she was observing the group from her usual spot near the door, the dance teacher saw her and asked her to come inside.

Vimla nervously stepped inside the room with her head bent down, unsure whether she would be told off for lurking around uninvited and secretly watching the group practice all this while. She walked to where the woman was standing and stood in front of her. The dance teacher then asked, 'What's your name, child?'

'Vimla', she replied back meekly, shifting her feet around nervously.

'Don't be afraid, I am not here to scold you', the woman said kindly. 'Look up Vimla, do you like to dance?'

Vimla raised her eyes slightly to look the woman in her eyes, and gave the tiniest of nods.

'Well… I know you like to dance because I have seen you looking at us practice for the past few days now. I thought you would gather up the courage to come inside one of these days, but seeing as you were determined to stay hidden, I decided to call you in instead', the teacher said, her voice overtly sweet. That the teacher had known that Vimla had been secretly watching them practice and that she was not angry made Vimla more comfortable around the woman and felt she could trust her now, so she afforded a sheepish grin.

'Well don't just stand there with that ludicrous smile on your face, show us what you can do', the teacher said, and with that she handed over a pair of *ghunghroo*s to Vimla and stood back.

A little taken aback at the upfront and sudden directive to dance, Vimla nevertheless took the *ghunghroo,* wore it around her ankle and stood up facing the woman and her dozen or so students, who were all looking at Vimla expectantly. Hoping she wouldn't make a fool of herself, Vimla started dancing; slowly and carefully in the beginning, but then picking up her pace as she began to lose herself in the movements and let go of all her inhibitions, like she most often did while dancing. The entire room was silent save for the sound of the *ghunghroo*s as Vimla danced and danced, giving all her heart and soul into the performance and only stopped when she thought she could go on no longer. Catching a stitch on the side of her stomach

and drawing huge heaves of breath, Vimla looked at the teacher, waiting for her to say something.

'Well that was... from the heart. I am so happy that you found us!' the woman exclaimed, walking towards Vimla and patting her affectionately on her head.

'Th-thank you ma'am', panted Vimla, still out of breath.

'You should join the class and learn how to dance along with the rest of the girls. You obviously have fire and desire in your heart, but it needs to be honed and channelled properly before you can become a good dancer', the woman said. She then asked her, 'Who are you here with? Are your parents here?'

'No, but I have come with my elder sister. She takes music lessons in the other classroom', Vimla replied back.

'Oh I see. Why don't you bring her here and I will talk to her', the dance teacher told Vimla.

Thrilled at the prospect of taking dance lessons, Vimla ran back to her sister's class and dragged Indu with her to meet the dance teacher.

'What was so important that you couldn't even wait for me to finish my lessons?' asked a slightly annoyed and flabbergasted Indu, as the two walked towards the dance class with Vimla leading the way.

'You will see *di*, just come with me', came back Vimla's reply, breaking into a trot as they neared the classroom.

'This had better not be a waste of my time. I swear, if this is another of your stupid prank.... ohh', Indu broke off as she saw Vimla standing by the door of the class where girls took dance lessons, realising what her sister was up to. Beckoning her sister to come fast, Vimla entered inside.

'Ma'am, that's my elder sister Indu', Vimla said to the teacher, pointing towards the door where Indu was just entering.

Indu walked towards the teacher and said politely, 'I am sorry ma'am if she has been bothering you', looking towards Vimla. 'My sister has a habit of being inquisitive.'

'Bothering me? No, no. You've got it all wrong. Let me first introduce myself. My name is Kavita and I am the dance instructor around here', she said, waving at the class they were in. She then continued, 'Vimla here has a real flair for dancing, and I would like to take her under my wing and train her in classical dance along with the rest of my students. She said you take music lessons here, which is why I asked her to bring you to me so I could talk to you'.

'Train her in classical dance?' repeated an unsure Indu. 'I think she is a little too young for it, ma'am.' Vimla was ten years old.

'On the contrary, this is the perfect age for her to start', Kavita insisted. 'She has the potential to become an excellent dancer and it would be unwise to not encourage that.'

‘I don’t know whether our father will be too pleased with Vimla taking dance lessons. He has his…er…reservations about things like dance and music’, stated Indu.

‘But aren’t you also taking music lessons? It seems all your father needs is a little convincing’, said Kavita, with a nod and a wink towards Indu. Before she could say anything back in protest, Kavita added in an affirming tone, ‘I hope the next time you’re here for your music class you will drop Vimla off for her first lesson in classical dance’.

Later that night at home, with a little help from Rani, Indu and Vimla were able to convince their father to let Vimla start taking dance lessons. ‘I don’t know what you girls are playing at, wanting to dance and sing. You might as well quit your studies’, Shastri had fumed, before giving in to his youngest daughter’s whim.

From then on, Vimla and Indu would regularly go after school hours for their respective classes in dance and music. Over the course of time, the two had become really proficient in their respective fields and would make an excellent pair; Indu would sing while playing a *dholak* or a *sitar* and Vimla would don on a pair of *ghunghroo*s and dance to her sister’s tunes. The duo would often practice together and had started to perform at various functions and occasions for which they both were appreciated and encouraged by those who saw them in their act. Those were perhaps some of the best years in

Vimla's life; a time where she was truly able to live carefree without a worry in the world and enjoyed indulging herself in activities that directly spoke to her heart.

VIMLA OF THE WANDERING MIND

VIMLA THUS SPENT most of her teens engrossed in music, dance and movies. The little time she found outside of this was spent outdoors roaming around or playing with her neighbourhood friends. Whenever the topic of her studies, marks or future would be brought up by her father or her elder brothers, especially Dinesh who was more concerned about Vimla than anyone else, she would just casually brush it aside saying things like, 'My future will take care of itself' or 'I don't need to worry, things will fall into place on its own'.

But whether *she* did or not, her father worried a lot about Vimla who, now fourteen years old, was fast approaching the time every parent prepares for since the birth of their daughter; their marriage. To that end, he was concerned about her consistently poor results in school, her utter lack of interest in studying or anything to do with education and her indifference towards her future, but most of all, he was concerned about Vimla's constant complains of headaches whenever he would try and force her to sit and study.

It had started a few years ago when Vimla would complain of a ringing sound in her ears, accompanied by headache whenever she sat down to study. At the time, Shastri had dismissed her grumblings, thinking she was just making excuses to get out of studying. But she persisted with her story, saying that even in school, it was difficult for her to concentrate on lessons as every time she tried doing so, her head would start aching, as if someone was reaching into her brains through her ear canals and pulling on her wirings.

Vimla's strife with her headaches grew to such an extent that her father felt it prudent for them to get a medical opinion on the matter. He consulted with his eldest son Dinesh, who had completed his MBBS and was preparing to do MD, on what the right course of action should be. And so, on the recommendation of one of Dinesh's colleagues, they both took Vimla to see Dr PK Chowdhary, a neurologist at a hospital on the outskirts of the town.

Upon reaching the hospital, Dinsesh did all the talking for the appointment with the receptionist while Vimla waited along with her father, after which the three proceeded to the third floor where the doctor's chamber was. They entered the waiting room and Shastri and Dinesh took seats near the chamber, while Vimla slowly walked around the

room looking at the various charts and diagrams of the human skull and brain hung on the walls, fascinated by the many different representations of the most important organ of the human anatomy. After a while, she returned to join her father and her brother and sat beside them.

Children, who in their innocence are not yet sensitised to death and loss, tend to get carried away when thinking of possible ailments. Vimla was no different, and as they were sitting outside the doctor's chamber waiting for their turn, she tugged at her father's shirt and asked with the nonchalance of an unassuming child, 'Papa, do you think I could have brain cancer or a tumour?' Before her father could recover from the gravity of her casual question, Dinesh said angrily, 'Shut up silly girl! Enough of your nonsense. I'm sure what you have is nothing more than a simple case of migraine. Don't let me catch you saying something like this ever again'.

If there was anyone else in the family who Vimla feared apart from her father, it was her eldest brother. And so, after Dinesh's reprimand, Vimla sat quietly in her seat with her head bent low until the nurse called out her name and the three walked into the room to settle once and for all whether what Vimla had been suffering from for all these years was indeed a simple case of migraine or something much, much more serious.

As they entered the chamber, Dinesh walked

right up to the desk where the doctor was sitting, and extending his arm to introduce himself said, 'Hello Dr Chowdhary, my name is Dr DC Tyagi'. The doctor took his hand and gave a polite smile. Dinesh continued, pointing towards Vimla and his father, 'This is my father, and that's my younger sister Vimla. It is her we have come to get checked up. A friend of mine, who speaks very highly of you, recommended you to me'.

Dr Chowdhary nodded at the remark, and then looking at Vimla said, 'Come here child, take a seat'. Vimla walked towards the stool he pointed towards which was kept right beside his desk, and sat there timidly, looking at her father unsurely as he and Dinesh took seats opposite the doctor's desk.

'So tell me, what is the problem', the doctor asked Vimla.

Vimla again looked at her father, a little unsure of what to say. Leaning forward into the table, Shastri said to the doctor, 'She actually has been suffering from recurring headaches every time she sits down to study or concentrate on some other school work. At first, we thought she was faking it to get out of having to study. But it seems to have gotten more regular and worse now. We were hoping you could take a look at her and see what the problem is'.

Dr Chowdhary listened to what the man had to say, and then turned to Vimla to ask the same question again, 'So tell me girl, what is the

problem? And no need to be afraid, I want you to be completely frank and honest with me'.

Vimla again looked at her father, but then turned to the doctor and said, 'I don't want to study doctor. Every time I do that, it feels like my head is going to split. I really am not able to concentrate on my chapters for long as my head starts aching so bad, and I also feel this very annoying ringing sound in my ears. I am fine when I am doing other things, like household chores or listening to music or watching movies etc., but whenever I am in class listening to my teachers or at home trying to do my homework, I feel like my brain is getting worked up and my head will explode'.

The doctor listened to Vimla patiently and intently as she told him about her problems. Vimla felt really relieved and glad that someone was listening to her problems for the first time without interrupting her or saying that she was making it up. And so she went into even further detail about how her head ached, tracing her fingers along her skull to point out to the doctor how she felt the pain was most acute at times.

Dr Chowdhary then asked Vimla, 'Are there certain times in the year where you feel your headaches get worse. For instance, do you feel that you have a harder time during winters than during summer?'

Confused as to why he was asking this, Vimla replied, 'No, it is the same ever since I have started having these headaches'.

'Hmm, and do you have any trouble breathing? Do you get out of breath easily?'

Again Vimla replied in the negative, confused by what this had to do with her headaches.

The doctor merely nodded this time. He then took out his stethoscope and did a routine check-up of her pulse, after which he also measured her blood pressure. He then took out a small flashlight and shone it first inside Vimla's ear canals, and then up her nostrils and finally down her tonsils. Then turning towards Shastri and Dinesh, he announced, 'I need to run some tests on her before I can conclusively come to a diagnosis'.

Having kept quiet all this while, Dinesh chipped in, 'Do you feel that's necessary doctor? I mean for all we know it could be a simple case of migraine'.

The doctor looked Dinesh up and down, and gave a measured reply, 'It certainly is not a case of migraine. This could be more serious but we need to run some tests before coming to any conclusions'.

Taking out a pen from his pocket, he started scribbling something on the prescription sheet. He then handed the sheet of paper to her father and said, 'I have written down a few tests that she needs to do. First is a simple X-Ray of the skull to ascertain whether there is any physical damage or sign of a trauma to the brain. The second test is called a cerebral angiography. It helps examine the blood vessels in the brain so that we can

determine whether there is any injury to the brain or any such abnormalities like aneurysms. And lastly, she needs to do a neurotransmitter test by providing her urine samples which is important to understand the chemical imbalances, if any, in her brain. You can get the X-Ray done and provide urine sample for the neurotransmitter test today itself. But you'll have to come at a later date for the angiography as it typically takes three to four hours for the procedure and so she'll have to spend some time in the hospital itself. I am booking an appointment for the angiography for Friday, which is four days from now, by which time the results for the neurotransmitter test will also be here. So, you come back with her on Friday and then, with all three results in hand we'll be in a better position to give a diagnosis'.

Shastri took the sheet of paper with the tests written down, and then looking at the doctor asked, 'Where can we get these tests done?'

'There is a lab down the corridor on this floor itself. You can get the X-Ray and neurotransmitter test done there. Just hand them over this paper and they'll take over from there', Dr Chowdhary replied.

Standing up, Shastri took the doctor's leave, and the three exited the chamber and made their way past the waiting hall and into the corridor, walking towards where the lab was after getting directions from one of the hospital staff. With the sheet of paper clutched in his hand, Shastri entered the

lab, closely followed by Vimla and Dinesh, where he handed it over to the person sitting behind the counter. He took a minute to study the contents of the paper and then said, 'We'll do the X-Rays first'. With that, he beckoned Vimla to follow him to an anti chamber which was separated by the main room by a green curtain. The process took a little over ten minutes, something that took Vimla by surprise as she was expecting the X-Ray test to be a lot more dramatic than it actually was. From the sound of it, she had thought X-Rays were very powerful things and manifested in some physical form and getting a test done would be very exciting. But as it turned out, it was rather dull and a little painful as the slate on which she was supposed to keep her head was hard and uncomfortable and on top of that, she had to hold her head still and at awkward angles while the guy moved the big machine over her head several times.

Next was the urine test, which although was a straightforward process, had Vimla embarrassed when the guy handed over to her a small cylindrical container and asked her to collect her pee in it. However, she went to the washroom and did the needful, after which the guy took the sample and then asked them to come after a few days to collect the test results.

Father, daughter and son then left for home, for there was nothing more to do other than wait till Friday for the results to come which could shed

some light on why, of the nine children in the Tyagi household, Vimla was the only one with an ongoing animosity towards studies.

The week went by in an uneventful blur of usual activities, and Friday saw the trio tread the now familiar path back to the hospital, up the stairs and into the waiting hall, where they awaited the impending judgement.

Vimla felt an uneasy squirm creeping into her stomach and slowly make its way to her heart, of the kind she often felt before her exams in school when she feared failing the test. And it didn't help either that Vimla had come on an empty stomach, as were the doctor's instructions. Sitting there at the waiting hall, Vimla couldn't help having a similar feeling of failing this test, although she knew that for once, there was nothing she could do about it. They didn't have to wait too long for their turn, and when Dr Chowdhary saw the familiar faces of Vimla and her companions. He gave a soft smile and asked her, 'So, how are you feeling today? I hope you are ready for the test?'

Vimla gave a meek 'yes' for a reply and tried returning the doctor's smile, but her face showed her nervousness. 'There's nothing to be worried about, child. It is a very simple test and won't take much time', Dr Chowdhary said warmly, trying to calm down Vimla's nerves.

He then stood up from his seat and exited the room, but not before waving the three to follow his lead. Dr Chowdhary led them towards the same lab where they had gotten Vimla tested a few days back. He gave Vimla's file to the attendant sitting behind the counter and asked him to prepare the X-Ray table. Then turning towards Shastri and Dinesh, he explained the procedure, 'A cerebral angiography is not much different from getting an X-Ray done, except for this test, we will be using a dye which will act as a contrast material that will enable us to visualise the arteries and veins in her brain. For this purpose, we will be inserting a catheter through the artery in the groin and pass it all the way up to the neck. It's actually not as bad as it sounds, but still we will be putting her on a mild sedation so that she doesn't feel any discomfort during the entire process'.

He then paused and looked at the father-son duo enquiringly to see if they had understood the process and whether they had any questions, and when neither of them said anything, he gestured towards Vimla to proceed behind the curtain.

For the second time in her life, Vimla entered the small anti chamber which now looked a little different from the last time she had been here. It even smelled different from last time. There was another table beside the bed, on which was kept a large tray that housed several different instruments and object.

'We'll start the process now, ok? Please lie down on the bed and relax', said Dr Cowdhary, smiling at her again. Vimla did as she was told. 'We will give

you an injection now that will make you feel a little sleepy. It is so that you don't feel any discomfort during the test.' Vimla nodded. She felt the prick of a needle on her wrist as the doctor gave her an IV injection, and no sooner had he pushed the syringe and injected her with its contents, Vimla felt a weird sensation spreading from her arms to her entire body.

After that, the rest of the process was a haze for Vimla as she was hardly able to comprehend the flurry of activities happening around her, and the next thing she knew she was being carried and then was put into a hospital bed. She lay there for a few hours, her head feeling dizzy still from the medication she had earlier received. While she lay there, she had been given food and drinks that helped her feel slightly better. Dinesh was sitting on a chair beside the bed, but as far as she could tell, her father was nowhere to be seen. Vimla assumed he must be sitting with the doctor, going over her results with him – like the countless number of times he had sat with her teachers and gone over her results with them.

Another hour passed before their father walked into the room, closely followed by Dr Chowdhary. They strode their way towards Vimla's bed and while Shastri stood there, with his usual stoic expression that made it difficult for Vimla to guess whether the news was good or bad, Dr Chowdhary asked her kindly, 'So how are you feeling now?'

Now considerably at ease, Vimla replied, 'I feel better'. Then she asked the doctor warily, 'Are my test results in? Did I do well?'

Dr Chowdhary did not immediately reply. He then said, slowly and carefully, 'Well the good things is, you are in no immediate danger of anything. However, there is a slight complication inside your brain which is the reason why you are having those headaches. We could do a surgery to treat the complication, but your father and I discussed that it would be better to not go ahead with that option. For your headaches though, I have prescribed a few medicines that you can take if it becomes too much to bear, but then you will actually have to make a few changes in your routine and live life a little differently from now onwards. I have explained everything to your father, and you can ask him about it all when you reach home'. He then smiled at her and patting her shoulders lightly, added, 'For now, you are free to go'.

For Vimla, Dr Chowdhary's explanation had given rise to more questions than answers but she knew she wouldn't be given further answers until they had reached home. So, she thanked the doctor for his service and the three then headed back home, each one of them having an entirely different thought process running in their head.

'What do you mean she will have to leave school?' Rani asked her husband incredulously, unable to believe what he was saying. Here was a man who

had spent his entire life in pursuit of education and trying everything to ensure his children followed suit as well, and he was now proposing that his youngest daughter stop her education. 'What did the doctor say? Is Vimla alright?' she asked, a faint trace of panic now evident in her voice.

Vimla, who stood in the room, and was finally getting to hear what her father and the doctor must have discussed in the hospital earlier, could not believe her ears either.

Apparently, all those years back when she was down with typhoid, a complication had arisen in her brain for some reason. The doctor presumed it to be because of something called pneumonia, although she wasn't sure what it was. It had resulted in some sort of a clot in her brain which prevented a stable flow of blood to a portion of her brain. This was the reason why she would hear that ringing noise in her ears and why her head would act as though it wanted to separate itself from her body.

But the unbelievable part for her was her father saying, in his own words no less, that they needed to let Vimla ease up on her studies, that there was *no need* for her to stress with her school work anymore.

'You don't understand. The doctor said the only way to treat this would be to do a brain surgery. Do you realise how dangerous and risky that is, never mind how expensive?' Shastri told his wife. 'He said it was in Vimla's best interest, and ours too,

that she is not to focus on her studies any longer. If she tries to concentrate too hard on her books and takes too much of a stress, she will run the risk of further causing damage to the arteries in her brain. In any case, there is so much more to life than just studying and reading books', he said, though not sounding too sure of himself.

'Hah', Rani scoffed, 'you're saying this?' She then asked, worryingly, 'But then what is she supposed to do with her life?'

'We'll teach her to be adept at other things, the practical aspects of life; like household chores', he replied. 'And hope that we can find her a kind and loving husband who will appreciate her for the person she is, rather than go for her educational qualifications.'

'That is all fine. But don't you think it is a little too drastic for us to cut her off from school right away? Maybe we should at least let her study till standard X. It's a matter of less than two years. She need not stress herself with her school work; just get passing marks so that she can at least be called a 10th pass', Rani suggested.

Shastri considered Rani's words for a moment, and then said, 'Yes, I think you are right. It would be better if we let her study till at least class X'.

And so, it was decided that Vimla would attend another two years of school, but with minimal stress. Her father met with her teachers the following day and explained to them her condition. The teachers,

who held Shastri in high regard, heeded his request and allowed Vimla to sit in the classroom without actually her having to pay attention to the lessons. Her homework was also set such that she would be able to do them with less of effort put in.

Not used to being given such freedom from authorities who usually tried to restrict her every other activity, Vimla felt the developments around her to be quite surreal. For her part, she did not at all mind the slack given to her in school, and merrily went along with the drill and continued living her life like she had grown used to; carefree, lost in her own world and doing the things she loved like dancing and listening to music.

Where earlier she had to force herself to sit behind her books for fear of her father's scolding, now she would confidently roam around the house without so much as giving her books a second look for days on end, having been given the license to do so. However, with all the extra time she now had at hand, her mother had started asking her to contribute in household chores. So, she was now doing everything, from cooking, washing clothes and cleaning the house to grocery shopping and managing the house along with her mother. Still, she enjoyed all of that, way more than she had studying, and would trade household work for reading a book any day.

And, so it continued for Vimla like this for another few years. Given how little time and interest she spared towards her studies, it came as no surprise to either Vimla or her parents when she failed to clear her school final examinations more than once. As a result, Vimla was nineteen years old by the time she got into class X. However, the fact that she took more time than others to complete her education did not bother Vimla the slightest; she continued to be her usual merry self and took life in its stride as it came along.

But all that was to change when on one afternoon, after returning from school, she saw two strangers from the window of her house sitting inside their living room, talking to her eldest brother Dinesh. She did not know it then, but she had seen for the first time the man she was going to get married to.

VIMLA, ON BUTTERFLY WINGS

DINESH WAS A socialising man, and over the years Vimla had gotten used to the idea of her elder brother having guests over at their house. She was also used to the idea of being more or less unacknowledged at her own house when he had guests, since Dinesh preferred being left alone with his friends. And so, she had learned to ignore their presence beyond just customary greetings on those rare occasion when her brother introduced her to his friends, which in all her years of existence had hardly happened more than three or four times.

When she saw from outside the two strangers sitting in their living room, Vimla had already started tracing her steps towards the back entrance of their house so there would be no unintended interruptions on her part. So, it came as a big surprise to her when, as she was making her way from the kitchen and into her room, Dinesh greeted her and said, 'So, you have come back from

school, hmmmm. Come with me, let me introduce you to my friends'.

Bewildered, Vimla asked, 'You want me to meet your friends? Why?'

'You just come with me, don't bother yourself with the whys and why nots', came back Dinesh's impatient reply.

Indu, who had only arrived the day before from her in-law's place – and was standing near the door when she saw Vimla entering the house – said, '*Bhaiya,* don't you want her to change into fresh clothes first? She has just come back from school. Let her at least wash her face before you introduce her to them'.

'I don't understand the fuss you are making about this', Dinesh told Indu. Looking towards Vimla, he added, 'Change your kurta and come, but be quick about it'.

'No, no, let me make her wear a saree', Indu insisted.

'No need for that. If you want to change the kurta that's fine, nothing else. They have been waiting for so long, don't delay this any further than you have to', Dinesh said and turned around to head back into the living room without waiting for a reply, marking the finality of his statement.

Vimla, who had been a silent but confused spectator to this weird exchange between her elder siblings, turned to Indu and asked, 'What is all this about? Why is *bhaiya* so keen on introducing me to his friends?'

‘Come with me’, Indu said, walking back into the room, ‘and close the door behind you’. Vimla followed, her gait giving away the uncertainty of the situation she was feeling.

Once inside, Indu smiled at Vimla and said, her voice high, ‘Silly girl, haven’t you caught on yet? Those two men sitting outside? They have come here with a marriage proposal for you. In fact, one of them might be your future husband!’

‘What!’, Vimla said wide eyed, matching the pitch of her sister’s voice.

‘Yes’, Indu replied, laughing at the look on her sister’s face. ‘Now come here and change into the best kurta you have.’

Vimla, who was still comprehending the reality of the situation, was rooted to her spot. She knew this day would eventually come ever since Manju had gotten married. She had, in fact, been excited at the prospect whenever she would dreamily think of getting married, for the idea of meeting some unknown person and starting a new life together in a faraway land had seemed rather fascinating.

But now that the prospect had knocked at her door and had presented itself right in front of her, Vimla felt oddly uneasy. Perhaps it was the shock of the news and the unexpected arrival of it that made Vimla feel this way, but she nevertheless dragged her way across the room and towards her cupboard, where she took out a crisp blue kurta which she always liked wearing. As she started changing into

fresh clothes, she felt more at ease with herself. After she was ready, she looked at Indu for assurance.

'You look really pretty', chimed her elder sister. 'Although I wish bhaiya had given us some time to change you into a saree and redo your hair', sighed Indu.

But Vimla afforded a smile, for now she felt confident and sure of herself. And as she started walking towards the living room, she could feel in her stomach the caterpillar of uneasiness evolving into a little butterfly of excitement. With a soft smile planted on her face, Vimla walked into the room where the two men were sitting with her brother, now joined by her father and mother as well.

One of them was talking to her father, while the other was listening to something Dinesh was saying; Rani was not a part of either conversation and just sat there quietly. Vimla's appearance at the doorway made the four men suspend their activities mid-air, and all five heads including Rani's turned in sync to silently welcome to the room the person whose presence had been anticipated and felt by its occupants even before she began tracing the first steps that led her here.

'There's my youngest daughter, our munni', announced Shastri happily to no one in particular. 'Hello', said Vimla cheerfully to the two men who had now stood up to greet her, and then without breaking her stride or waiting for a reply, she swiftly walked by them and promptly sat between

her father and mother. After the two men had sat down as well, one of them said, 'Hello, my name is Solanki. And this is my friend Devendra'. Vimla nodded in acknowledgment to him and then turned her eyes on his friend, waiting for some introduction from his end, but when none came she turned her attention back to the first person.

After an initial moment of hesitation followed by uncomprehending murmur in the air, Solanki resumed his conversation with their father, although Vimla did not catch a word of what they were saying since they were conversing in English and she had no knowledge of the language. From time to time, he would look at Vimla, staring at her longer than she felt appropriate, but instead of being shy about it and lowering her own eyes, Vimla glared back indignantly. She kept waiting for a chance to say something when he would ask her about herself, but it never came, and his conversation with her father continued in a stream of words that went past her faster than a speeding bullet.

Vimla still listened intently, as if her fate hung in the balance on their conversation and her paying attention to it was of vital importance in the determination of its outcome. Their fluid exchange was interrupted occasionally by Dinesh, who would add something to the ongoing conversation. Vimla noticed the fourth person sitting quietly, with his eyes fixed on the ground the entire time, as though he too was an outside party to a conversation that,

like her, he could not follow.

After some while, Shastri excused himself and got up to leave the room, thinking it prudent for his children to have some time to talk amongst themselves as well.

He looked at Rani, indicating she too should follow his lead and walk out. Seeing both her parents leaving, Vimla also began getting up but was immediately rebuked by Dinesh who said, 'Where are you going? You stay here'. Vimla acquiesced without a word. He then waited for a couple of minutes for their guests to talk to her or ask something of her, but was only met with an awkward silence following which he said to Vimla, 'Why don't you go and get us some tea'. Vimla again obliged and without a word got up, turned around and headed towards the kitchen, but not before giving Solanki, who had his eyes fixed on her, one last stony glance.

She went inside the kitchen, her head swimming with thoughts of the encounter she just had with her prospective husband. She was not sure whether what she felt within was of a positive nature, for she certainly did not feel that way. But she busied herself with making tea for them, trying to ward off any bitter feeling that occupied her mind and hoping that the second encounter would yield a better result and change the way she felt about him. As she was straining the tea from the saucepan into the cups, she thought about the leftover tea leaves

that sat at the bottom of the utensil – black, used and unwanted; the most essential element which gives tea its flavour now leeched of its own essence and devalued to its core, lying at the bottom to be thrown away.

She wondered if that's how her life would be like in the end; used, drained and disposed. Not sure why her mind was being visited by such gloomy thoughts, she nevertheless arranged the cups on a tray and carried it to the living room, determined to make her second meeting more fruitful.

However, when she walked into the living room she found the place empty. She put the tray down at the table and went outside to see if they had perhaps stepped out for some fresh air. On finding no sign of either her brother or the two men, she came back inside and went to her parent's room and asked them quizzically, 'Where did *bhaiya* and his friends go?' 'We don't know child. Weren't you with them?' came back her father's reply in an even more quizzical note. 'Never mind', said Vimla and exited the room brusquely so that she was already outside when she heard her mother's voice tailing behind her asking, 'So, how did you like the boy?' But she ignored the question, as she was ignoring it inside her own head, and walked straight into her room. She saw Indu sitting on her bed and knew instantly from the look on her sister's face what her first words were going to be.

And sure enough, Indu asked, her eyes

twinkling, 'So my dear little sister, you have danced a lot to the tunes of my music. How did you like the man to whose tune you will now have to dance for the rest of your life?'

'*Di,* I am really sceptical. I don't have a good feeling about this', Vimla blurted out.

Dropping her earlier impish tone, Indu asked, 'What do you mean? What is the matter? Did you not like the man? I thought he was rather well behaved'.

'I don't know how you gathered his behaviour to be good-natured. On the contrary, I felt his behavior was extremely rude towards me. I mean not in a direct sense where he said something rude to me, but the way he kept staring at me. It was so uncomfortable and annoying. Huh, what does he think of himself', said Vimla, her face flushed and her nostrils flared. 'Just because he can speak fluently in English doesn't mean he is automatically entitled to behave any way he pleases.'

'Wait a minute, who are you talking about', asked Indu, narrowing her eyes in suspicion.

'Who else, the man sitting across me who was talking to papa. That Solanki fellow.'

Indu smacked her forehead with the palm of her hand and said exasperatedly, 'You stupid girl! And here you had me worried for no apparent reason.'

'What do you mean?'

'Solanki was only a friend accompanying *your*

guy. You're supposed to get married to the other fellow, Devendra.'

'What?' exclaimed Vimla. 'The one who kept quiet the entire time? I thought he had come reluctantly and had been forced into this situation, seeing as he was not talking at all and had eyes only for the floor.'

'Probably because of you, my dear sister. He, in fact, was talking quite animatedly when they both first came to the house, while you were still on your way back from school. Moreover, and if I am not wrong, he left a very favourable impression upon papa.'

It was Vimla's turn to smack herself on her forehead as she said, 'I hardly even gave him a second glance since I thought I was supposed to get married to the other person. I don't even remember how he looks!'

'You'll have plenty of opportunities to get a proper look at him once you two get married', Indu said with a wink.

'Oh *diiii*. Stop it, will you', Vimla sighed. 'But yeah, I guess you're right', she eventually muttered after a short pause.

The previous reservations which Vimla had towards getting married to someone she did not like was now replaced with a curious sense of assurance, even though she hardly knew anything about Devendra, the person she now *knew* was going to be her husband.

She obviously felt assured in the fact that her

father and her brother had her best interests in her heart and would find her the right match, but there was also her intuitive feeling which made her, for some unknown reason, think of her future husband in a positive light. Trying hard to remember something, anything about him and cursing herself for being so self-absorbed that she remembered nothing other than his friend's conduct, Vimla walked out of her room and planted herself in a chair in the living room, waiting for her brother's return so she could seek answers to questions she already felt she had no doubts about.

Meanwhile, Dinesh had taken his two guests to a nearby hotel for some tea and snacks and more importantly, to ascertain whether they liked what they saw of Vimla or not. But even before Dinesh had picked up his cup to take the first sip of tea, Devendra blurted out his admission to liking Vimla and gave his assent to the marriage. Solanki too agreed with his friend, nodding his approval.

Dinesh was overcome with happiness as he heard Devendra give his consent. His enthusiasm spilled over as he took Devendra's hand and shook it rather firmly. Without loosening his grip on Devendra's hand, he then proceeded to tell him how Vimla was almost like a daughter to him; she was the youngest girl in the house and so had been raised with great love, care and pampered. Devendra said reassuringly not to worry about Vimla now, and that he would try to keep her life

with him as happy and fulfilled as it had been with her family.

After this initial exchange of niceties, Dinesh did not want to hide anything or leave any room for future doubts and so he also told Devendra everything about Vimla's injury to her brain and her struggles with education. Devendra was very understanding of it and seemed hardly bothered by the fact that his to-be wife was not as educated as her siblings or her father. He told Dinesh not to worry and irrespective of what he had just heard, he would still like to go ahead with marrying Vimla. He said it did not matter whether Vimla had any success with formal education or not, for the groundwork of the morals and values she held today had been laid long before she was born, when her father had chosen to walk down the path of education himself.

In fact, Devendra's initial interest in the proposal had arisen due to his understanding that his in-laws were from a well-educated background, for there was nothing Devendra valued more in life other than education. It did not matter to Devendra whether his in-laws were affluent or not and he cared little for materialistic wealth, for what mattered to him was only the wealth of knowledge. He felt that Vimla's family roots were so deeply entrenched in educational values that her own lack of it was not of much concern.

Dinesh was very pleased to hear his future

brother-in-law have such a progressive outlook. He had no further doubts about Devendra and whether he was the right man for his little sister, and he gave his blessings for them both to have a long and happy married life.

While her marriage was thus being fixed by her eldest brother, Vimla sat waiting in anticipation for him to get back home, unaware of the fact that her fate had already been sealed. She was now not sitting alone, as both her parents and Indu had joined her to wait for Dinesh's return. Indu, meanwhile, had also reheated the tea Vimla had made earlier for the guests, and the four of them now sat, each with a cup of tea in their hands. They sat in silence, save for the rhythmic slurping of tea, each running a separate train of thought.

Vimla sat with her legs folded up on the chair and back straight, straining her ears for any sign of her brother's arrival, unsure of what the future held for her. There was an uncertainty in her situation which made her uncomfortable and she did not like this feeling. This was completely opposite to how Vimla usually felt given her devil-may-care attitude towards life, and this irony was not lost on her. Where earlier she couldn't care less about the uncertainty of what lay ahead, for the first time in her life she cared about a future she was unsure of.

It was long after the last dreg of tea had been drained from Vimla's cup that she saw her brother approaching the house from the window of the

room. She sprung out of the chair and quickly walked across the room to open the door for him. Dinesh smiled when he saw his little sister waiting by the door for him, and he pulled her cheeks playfully with both his hands before walking in.

Vimla closed the door behind him and turned around to face her brother, leaning her back against the door, waiting for him to proclaim what fate awaited her.

Dinesh walked up to his father, put one arm on his shoulder and said simply, 'He said yes'. And then turned around to look at his youngest sister straight in her eyes as he repeated, 'He said yes munni. He said he likes you.'

As soon as Dinesh said this, everyone around Vimla burst out in a buzz of excitement. Both Rani and Indu came running towards Vimla, hugging her and planting kisses on her cheeks, crying their happiness on the news of her marriage being fixed. Shastri too walked up to his daughter, his lips pursed but his eyes reflecting all the happiness in the world, and patted her lovingly on the head before giving her a big hug.

Vimla, who was still internalising the news her brother had brought back, was quietly embracing all the love, hugs and kisses coming her way. She was not able to coherently comprehend all the things the people around her were saying, as her own head was buzzing with a hysterical frenzy. She was unquestionably elated by the news, and the

excitement she felt at the prospect of her marriage was undeniable, and yet she was unsure of how exactly to manifest these feelings in her physical disposition. So she stood still for a while, her back leaning against the door, not having moved since Dinesh had walked in, and then as suddenly she broke into a grin, blushed furiously and ran into her room with her face buried in her hands.

VIMLA'S DREAM TIME

THE MONTH FOLLOWING the news of her marriage was spent in a haze of dream and reality, for while Vimla was spinning yarns of her own imagination of what her married life would be like, she also had to simultaneously study for her class X matric examinations. She did not understand the fuss around the importance of her clearing this examination, just as she never did before. However, as was usually the case, she had to surrender her will to her father's and brother's commands when it came to her studies, and Dinesh had especially stressed on her passing her matriculation or there would be no question of her marriage.

Despite now Vimla having to forcefully sit herself down and study for her upcoming exams, she only had to look outside her window to see a reflection of what was really going on inside her. All around her there was a bloom of fresh buds, vines and flowers, signalling the arrival of summer and just like in the nature surrounding her, there was a pitter patter in Vimla's own gait and canter. She now moved with a lightness in her feet afforded only by the newly-smitten.

The month passed by in the flutter of a butterfly's wings, and Vimla saw herself preparing for her wedding with equal measure of fervour, excitement and anxiety. Her exams went surprisingly smoothly; perhaps it was the effect of Dinesh's warning, or perhaps it was the apparent haze in which she had given it that made her sail past the days with hardly any hiccups. Either way, she felt finally free from the shackles of education that had always felt like tying her down.

Now her days were spent in merrily roaming the markets with her mother and shopping for her wedding; evenings in happily gossiping with her neighbouring friends and sisters, mostly Indu, and conjuring wild ideas of what she will do once married; and nights giddily lying in bed trying to get some sleep but revisiting in her head all the thoughts and fantasies she had cooked up regarding married life. Whether it was a seasonal thing or whether she had only started noticing it now, but Vimla suddenly began spotting more and more couples walking hand in hand, infecting the air with their contagious laughter every time she went outside for a walk or for some work.

In the month preceding the wedding, Choudhary Chokhe Singh, who was a relative

of Vimla, had introduced Devendra's family to Vilmla's father. Devendra had earlier already seen Vimla in Kanpur and had given his nod for the marriage. The entire family went to Devendra's native village, along with her brother Dr Umesh Tyagi, to propose Vimla's marriage with Devendra, to Devendra's father. The father, it turned out, was curious to know from Chokhe Singh if the bride's family had brought 'something' to present as well. When Chokhe Singh had spoken to Vilmla's father in this regard he expressed his inability to pay anything because he wanted this wedding to happen as an 'ideal marriage'. Following his initial reluctance, Choudhary Chokhe Singh had managed to convince Devendra's father (perhaps after some forceful intervention from Devendra) to this alliance.

According to Umesh Tyagi, Devendra's bua (aunt) also played a very crucial role in convincing Devendra's father for this marriage. While Devendra's father displayed mild resistance during the discussion, buaji had asked the guests not to take Devendra's father's behaviour seriously and prophesied that 'these minor differences will be sorted out', which eventually happened.

The entire community regarded Devendra and Vimla's wedding as an 'ideal marriage'. Shastri, Dinesh and other relatives had twice visited Devendra's village, Khilwai, to meet him and his family. Vimla had learned through them that

Devendra had a job in Lucknow with the literacy department, that he had two brothers and four sisters, that his father was a *daaroga*, a police officer and that he was an overall affable and jovial person. The date for the marriage was fixed as 11th May, after consulting with *pandit*s and drawing up and matching with the relevant astrological charts, and they had decided to get Vimla married off not from Kanpur but from Shastri's ancestral village Garh Mukhteshwar, which was very close to Khilwai and, therefore, convenient for both the bride and the groom's families.

The month of May brought with it a wave of heat in both the weather and the Shastri family's temper as preparations for the wedding now had to begin in full swing. So a week before the wedding, Vimla, along with her parents and most of her siblings came to Garh Mukhteshwar to make proper arrangements for the groom and his family's arrival. Rakesh, Vimla's youngest brother, hadn't been allowed to come since his school exams were not yet over and Shastri was not going to let something like his sister's wedding come in the way of his examinations.

Umesh had opted to stay back on account of watching over his younger brother since there would be no one else at home and also because he had only recently joined work as a medical examiner in a hospital in Kanpur and did not want to take a leave of absence of one week so early into his medical career.

Shastri, who was coming back to his village after several years, did not have much of family left in Garh Mukhteshwar, and so he and his children were left with almost no means but themselves to try and make as best arrangements as possible for welcoming the groom's family. This was a very serious affair and was no easy task.

Traditions and rituals hold a very special and endearing place in the hearts and minds of millions of Indians, and they take these traditions very seriously. An important part of wedding traditions is the reception given to the groom's family and friends when they come to the bride's home where the wedding takes place. There have been countless instances of *baraatis* calling the wedding off, after having felt their reception at the hands of the bride's family had been lacking in grandeur or hospitality. And so it was important that Shastri had everything in order and to the liking of the *baraatis* when they came, to prevent any such untoward mishap from happening.

Meanwhile, Vimla's anticipation and excitement had reached feverish levels in the week leading up to the wedding. The days were lined up with several different functions and rituals, and Vimla was lapping up all the love and attention that came her way, as is due to any bride. Pre-wedding rituals in Indian weddings are as elaborate as the wedding itself – *Haldi, Mehendi, Sangeet, Achyuta* – and to not only be a part of these but at its centre is a dream every Indian girl grows up with, and Vimla

too grew up fantasising about them ever since she could remember.

She had no memory of when Prem had been married since she was only a year old then, but vividly remembered the marriage of her other two sisters, Indu and Manju. At the time, she had also wanted to paint her arms and legs yellow with turmeric but was told she would have to wait for her own marriage for that to happen. That day was finally here.

She felt goosebumps down her spine as her mother started applying the *haldi* paste on her face, arms and legs. She was similarly jubilant when it was time for the *mehendi* ceremony. Vimla had applied henna on her hands countless times before, but she could swear it had never looked as beautiful as it did now, sitting there and watching the slow, intricate and artistic progress of the elaborate design unfolding before her eyes. It was a weird feeling that night when she went to bed, for she knew this was the last night of her life as *herself*, and everything was to change come tomorrow.

Come tomorrow, Vimla woke up with the most radiant smile on her face. As she went about her day's activity – getting dressed mostly – the commotion around her seemed oddly muted. She had distanced herself from the fret and fuss of last-minute preparations which could be seen in the faces of the swirls of people running here and there. For Vimla, there was only the wedding on her mind, and for this brief moment nothing else

registered for her; not her parents, not her brothers or sisters, and not even who she was getting married to; only that it was her wedding day and she was the centre of the universe for this one moment. She would have liked this moment to linger forever, but even before she could close her eyes and savour it, she was being walked out of her room with a heavy veil placed over her head and led to the *mandap* to get married.

Vimla had not seen Devendra since their uneventful encounter in her house in Kanpur where they were first introduced to one another, and because she had paid little or no attention towards him at the time, she only had a fleeting memory of what he looked like. As she climbed her way on to the *mandap*, she saw Devendra sitting in front of the holy fire, his face indiscernible from behind the *sehra* he was wearing. Vimla slowly walked around the fire and took her place beside him. She tried getting a peek from underneath her own heavy veil but could barely see the side of his face, the rest covered in a curtain of flowers.

She realised suddenly that she was getting married to a man whose face was only a blurry memory to her, and so she did not even know for sure how he looked like. As she was thinking about this, someone from the crowd suddenly shouted, 'Lift her veil up and make sure she has a mole on her cheek to see if she is the right girl!' Such incidents where the groom ends up marrying the

wrong woman was quite common in villages, and so it was prudent to make sure you were marrying the right person. Devendra slowly lifted Vimla's veil and said brusquely, 'Yes, it's her only'. Vimla thought about her present situation, and wondered why rather, she shouldn't be the one lifting up *his* veil and checking to make sure *he* was the right person or not, but then she laughed the idea off in her own head. Vimla's father, however, was upset at this crude display of doubt.

It was evening by the time Vimla and Devendra had taken their seats next to each other beside the sacred fire. Shastri, who was a learned man and a Sanskrit scholar, had decided he would be the one performing the rites of the *pandit*, for he did not like the way some *pandit*s recited the prayers and *shloka*s. His distaste was particularly towards *pandit*s trying to wrap up the wedding ceremonies as soon as possible by cutting short certain rites or imperfectly pronouncing the Sanskrit *shloka*s in their haste.

Therefore, when Shastri took his place at the head of the fire and started leading the bride and groom to perform each step along the way as guided by tradition, he made sure they did so meticulously and down to a T. It took almost 3 hours for him to thus complete all the rites and rituals as stipulated by Hindu traditions. When Vimla and Devendra finally stepped off from the *mandap,* they did so together and for the first time as husband and wife;

the sun had set for the day, but for Vimla it was a new beginning.

That new beginning, however, turned out to be long-drawn out. For some reason, the *baarat* had left for Khilwai without taking the bride and groom with them. Only Devendra and his friends had stayed back. Vimla recalled snatches of conversation, 'doli nahin uthayaa', ... they had not taken the bride with them. She also heard that her father had run short of cash as he did not live in the ancestral village and was not able to immediately provide the amount of cash the groom's party had demanded. He had provided his daughter the traditional *streedhan*, clothes, jewellery, household gifts but no dowry.The groom's party from the adjacent village had claimed, they had not been 'properly' looked after. The new extended family she had embraced had, therefore, left Garh Mukhteshwar immediately after the 'phera' or the going-round-the-fire ceremony. They remained cold and aloof long afterwards, until Devendra took her away to the city.

'Take care of yourself and be careful not to bother anyone in your new home.'

'I will miss you so much, now who is going to pester me into taking them to the cinemas to watch a movie?'

'Write to us every week and let us know if you are having any problems adjusting with your new family members.'

'We had a good run, you and I, playing music and dancing together. Life is never going to be the same again. I wish you all the strength for dealing with the ups and downs that come with the unpredictability of future.' That was Indu, the sister, who had an unhappy marriage.

All this and more were being said as Vimla was drowned in an exchange of tears, hugs and embraces that belied the happiness she actually felt inside. Yes, she was sad for the fact of having to leave her parents and siblings and to go live with an entirely new set of people who she had no idea how they were like, but she was equally welcoming of it. The prospect had always excited her, and it was not going to change now when she finally had to do it. After all the farewells had been said and tears shed, Vimla was finally on her way to Khilwai with Devendra and his friends.

Vimla was sitting with Devendra on the back of a cart being pulled by a horse, the same horse he had been escorted on as a groom with the *baraati*s while on his way from Khilwai. The rest of his family and friends followed suit in bullock carts, while some had even come on bicycles and were now hustling along with the rest of the party. She sat quietly, waiting for him to break the silence and say something. But Devendra had his eyes fixed on the road ahead, and as soon as they turned away from the village and got onto the main highway, he took off his turban and kept it aside. He then

turned towards her and said with a grin on his face, 'I never expected your father to be the *pandit* for our wedding. I thought the ceremony would take at the most half an hour to complete, but he continued non-stop for three hours!'

He then added, 'You can take your veil off you know. You wouldn't want to miss out on the lovely breeze in this hot weather'.

VIMLA IN A DAZE

WHEN VIMLA WOKE up the following morning she could feel a nervous excitement rising inside of her. She was not sure what to expect, and she began her day with bated breath in anticipation of how the events of the day would unfold for her. The previous night Devendra had dropped her off at the house and had told her he would see her later the next day. The household setup in the village was such that all the women in a family would stay in the house, while the men would stay in another compound outside the house called the *gher*. Women were traditionally not allowed to go inside the *gher*, and so there was no way for Vimla to go and see Devendra unless he came to see her.

Slowly, anxiously, Vimla got out of her room which was on the first floor and headed downstairs from where she could hear noises coming. Vimla had not noticed how huge the house was last night as it was dark when she had come in. She could not help but be in awe at how big and spacious everything was. The courtyard, which was in the middle of the house and which she could see from the balcony upstairs, was large enough to fit in their Kanpur house, thought Vimla. She circled around the balcony to climb down the stairs and found her way to the kitchen where her mother-in-law was already there along with two of her sisters-in-law. She greeted them with a smile as she entered the kitchen, but as soon as her mother-in-law turned around to see who it was she immediately asked her to veil her face. It was tradition in those days for a bride not to show her face. Brought up in a city, Vimla had forgotten this. Vimla quickly pulled the fall of her saree over her head and covered her face which had turned into a deeper shade of red than her own saree, saying sheepishly, 'I'm sorry, I forgot'.

If Vimla had been unsure of what to do when she woke up in the morning, she was absolutely clueless as to what had just happened and what she should do next. Transfixed, she stood there in the kitchen wondering whether she had inadvertently offended her mother-in-law and if she should go after her to offer a proper apology.

'Don't worry about it. You will get used to being around her in a few days. Ma means well.'

It was one of Devendra's sisters who Vimla had briefly met the previous night, although she still did not know one from another.

'Are you sure though? Should I not go after her

and say sorry once more?' asked Vimla timidly. 'I just...I have never had my face covered with a veil like this before. I did not know it was the norm here', she added, noticing that both the women in the kitchen had veils over their heads covering half their faces.

'Yeah you'll get used to that as well. It's really not that much of a trouble you know, and it's taken as a sign of disrespect if we come near our elders without our heads covered', said the woman who had spoken to her earlier.

She spoke softly and kindly, and even from under the veil Vimla could sense the gentle contours of her face and the pleasant smile that rested underneath it. The woman continued, 'I don't think we got a proper introduction yesterday. I'm Maya, and this is my younger sister Santosh', she said. Her friendly nature and gentle reassurances allayed Vimla's earlier trepidations, and she afforded a smile while greeting her two sisters-in-law. Maya then stepped towards Vimla and gently lifted up her veil to take a closer look at her.

'My, my, you are truly beautiful!', said Maya, who then wiped a little kajal off from underneath her right eye with her pinky finger and marked a small dot on Vimla's upper cheek to cast off any evil-eyes before covering her face back with the veil. 'Bhaiya is really lucky. May you both have a long and happy life together.'

'Thank you. You are very kind', said Vimla.

After a short pause she said flatly, 'I really don't know what I should do now. Your brother told me yesterday he would come see me today, but did not really mention when. Perhaps I should get dressed? Or if there's any help needed around the house tell me, I can lend my hand….'

'No, no, you go take a bath and get dressed. Let us worry about the household work for now. In any case, you are new here and it would take some getting used to before you start finding your way around here as comfortably as we do', Maya said, and then proceeded to lead Vimla by the hand and show her where the bathing area was. Vimla thanked her, and then after having gathered her clothes and other articles from her room went in for a bath. She then changed into a new saree which she had bought with her mother. While putting it on she remembered how excited she had been during those sessions of shopping around town and how carefully they had selected and bought each and every item for the wedding. And here she was now, sitting in her room with brand new clothes donned on but not a person around her to compliment her on how it looked. She stared into the dingy mirror that hung on the wall opposite where she was sitting, and a look of shocked disappointment stared back at her – with a sense of betrayal of her dreams, her fantasies and her emotions.

But she tried to ward off the gloom that was settling over her, and began thinking of brighter things like how it would be when Devendra would come to see her, where all they would go; perhaps they would go take a walk around the village and see the place around. After all, a long walk outside always seemed to cheer her mood up. So she started running down the clock, awaiting his arrival, looking forward to her day taking a positive spin – as she sat in her room, in between meals, while she walked up and down the house, during brief conversations with Maya – but Devendra never came to see her that day. He did not come to visit her the next day either and Vimla found herself in this new home with no real friends or family to turn to for comfort. What came instead was the foreboding gloom which had come back to haunt Vimla as she walked around the house restlessly, not sure what to do or how to pass her time.

On the third day, Vimla was visited by Devendra's grandfather who had come into the house to see her. He was the oldest member of the house and the patriarchal head of the family, and so everyone called him *baba*. He, in fact, was the one who had reached out to Shastri through an old link and came with the proposal for Vimla with his grandson. When Vimla came out to greet him, he was sitting on a cot in the middle of the courtyard. She saw his old profile through the veil covering her face; the arched back propped up as much as possible with the help of a bamboo stick which he held with his right hand, the wrinkled

skin hanging loosely on to his body from forehead to toes like the folds of clothes laying unattended, the wisps of white hair visible from underneath the turban he was wearing; but what struck her most was the glint in his eyes, sharp and alive as though unaware of the fragile body it belonged to. Vimla drew closer and bent down to touch his feet.

'Live long, child', said baba, placing his hand on top of her head to give his blessings.

'Wait here, I have something for you', he said, and then got up to proceed towards the kitchen, leaving Vimla wondering behind him. She stood there and watched him as he slowly made his way into the kitchen, and then emerged out from there carrying some things on a plate in his hand. He walked feebly back towards the cot, one hand holding the plate while the other holding the bamboo stick which seemed to be supporting the entire weight of his body. Fearing he would drop the plate on the floor, Vimla moved to help him carry it, but he held up his hand motioning her to stay where she was and continued at his own pace till he reached the cot where he sat down heavily, putting the plate down by his side.

As he put the plate down, Vimla was better able to see what its contents were. It had four items – a ripe mango, a raw mango, a potato and an onion. She wondered whether he meant for her to eat them or whether there was some other purpose behind bringing such a strange assortment of fruits and vegetables to her.

'Sit down', he told her. Vimla followed and sat down on the floor in front of him. He then handed over the plate along with a knife which he pulled from under his *kurti*. 'I want you to peel these', he said casually as though what he was asking of her was one of the most mundane things to do in the world. Concealing her look of surprise and confusion behind her veil, Vimla drew the plate near her and picked up the raw mango first. Slowly, carefully, she started peeling the mango, its chaff piling up on the floor until what lay in front of her was only the whitish-green raw pulp of the fruit, which she put back on the plate. She then took the onion, then the ripe mango and lastly the potato, peeling them one after the other. As she sat there peeling what had been given to her, Vimla felt strangely withdrawn from everything that had been bothering her until then and found herself squarely centred on the task at hand. Her single-minded focus would have put to shame the concentration with which any of her siblings sat down to study. She finally put down the potato and looked at the four items on the plate, now lying naked and exposed, baring what lay under their skin unlike Vimla, who still hid behind the curtain of her veil.

She picked the plate and held it up for baba's inspection, who had been watching all her movements closely, waiting for his verdict on how she had done. Baba took the plate from her and

put it down beside him on the cot, then he bent down and held Vimla by the side of her arms with a firm grip and said, 'My child, marriage is a bond for not only this life but for all seven lives. It is sacramental and should always be held with the highest regards in our hearts. I can tell that you are going to keep your family close and together, always. Not everyone is blessed with such a gift and you must cherish it, preserve it. May God bless you and bring you lots of happiness in your life'. With that, he got up to exit the courtyard and out the house, but not before taking with him the four peeled items which he put in his pocket.

Vimla sat there wondering at the meaning of all this, but feeling somewhat glad and content by his approval of her. His benign and gentle face had been the friendliest thing she had seen since leaving her own family behind, and it left with her an assurance that everything would pick up for her from now. The only thing left to do was for her to now see Devendra, and she knew all would be set right then. But as the day drew nearer to its end with no sign of Devendra, Vimla began fretting about uncomfortably again. She went to bed that night with a heavy heart and a despairing hope that perhaps tomorrow will bring with it a new dawn.

But dawn came without the hopes Vimla had set for herself, for Devendra did not come the next day either, or the day after that, or the day after that. Things had never looked so bleak for Vimla

as she went about her days with nothing better to do but aimlessly wander around the house. She was not much for staying indoors and craved to go outside for a walk but had been forbidden from leaving the house.

On top of it, she also felt suffocated for keeping a veil over her head at all times after having been reminded of it by her mother-in-law in no uncertain words when she caught her without it on one other occasion. This was an experience very unpleasant to Vimla's sensibilities, especially as she liked open spaces and unrestricted movements, and it had now started giving her headaches as well. She now felt all her dreams, all her hopes, all the fantasies of after-marriage life which she had cooked up disappearing in a waft of air that once echoed with the laughter of newly-wedded couples she had seen walking merrily in parks in Kanpur.

For nine days Vimla kept on like this. For nine days she stalked the walls of the house like a ghost, invisible and inaudible to its inhabitants save for a few short intervals of snap conversations here and there. She initially liked that nobody here seemed to be bothered with talking about books or studying, which was all everyone had to talk about at her own home. She even liked the refreshing change in taste which the village food brought for her, complete with copious amounts of *ghee* added to everything. But all of that quickly began waning as Vimla soon found herself being kept at a distance from

everything that was happening in the house. For, apart from being served her meals in her room and having access to use the bathroom as she pleased, Vimla was otherwise isolated from any usual activity that would make her feel part of a family.

During these nine days she caught snippets of conversations, some overheard, some intentionally said in front of her. She soon learnt that Devendra's uncle had not taken kindly to Vimla and had, on more than one occasion, stormed into the house to have heated discussions with the other members of the family. And although she would try to keep herself out of his sight, his words did not escape her ears. Vimla could not understand this hostility, and she definitely could not understand her part in aggravating it.

Of course, Vimla did not understand much of what exactly was happening. But from snatches of conversations she caught, she learnt that Devendra had been adopted by this uncle, whose child had died very young. To stem his grief, the family had given him Devendra, a younger child of his policeman brother.

The uncle thus thought, Devendra was rightfully his son, and he could dictate the terms of his marriage. He had brought another richer match, but Devendra's father had rejected it, because Devendra had chosen Vimla. The uncle did not like the family chosen to get the bride. He wanted a hefty dowry for Devendra.

Three proposals had come for the young man. One prospective bride's family had even sent a mountain of gifts to Devendra's house as a pre-nuptial commitment. Devendra had come home one evening and found the gifts laid out before him. He was furious and ordered his family to return everything at once as he was not going to marry that girl. Devendra's father was caught between his brother and his son. He was a daaroga, a typical British-era chief police constable, who had, perhaps not entirely honestly, amassed wealth, built a palatial house in the village, led a very comfortable life, wearing English clothes, listening to English music. Devendra was opposite of his father, very self-effacing although he was handsome to be selected for films and was considered a prize catch.

Devendra had been clear in his mind, he did not want a village girl. He had seen his elder brother's wife, whose only concern was getting mangoes from that garden, harvest from that field or gifts from this or that family of relatives. She was possessive about such acquisitions and kept count of how many mangoes who ate. Devendra was adamant about not getting into any liaison with any village family.

He had chosen Vimla because her family was from the city and she was the daughter and sister of learned people. He knew about Vimla's health condition, her learning disability, he still chose her for bride. He had also seen a beautiful young

woman, tall and slender, smiling, singing, dancing. He knew about his uncle's and father's greed. He did not want a dowry, he wanted a compatible wife.

Devendra was like his grandfather, who thought dowry-taking was a sin and marriage was a holy bond. On the sixth day, Vimla could hear the uncle abusing her father within her earshot. On the ninth day when Maya came to serve her lunch at her room, Vimla broke down and started crying incessantly. 'W-What are you d-d-doing to me? Why am I being t-t-treated this way?' Sobbing hysterically, she pushed aside the plate Maya had put down beside her. 'Am I here to only drink and eat, treated like a bloody prisoner no less!'

'Listen, the atmosphere around the house is slightly disturbed and everyone is tensed. It's not at all your fault, so please don't misunderstand the way everyone is treating you', said Maya, her voice low and sorrowful.

'What is there for me to misunderstand? I am not even able to understand what's happening. I came here thinking I am a newly wedded bride, so everyone would be excited and happy to have me around. But instead I am being shunned to a corner of the house like an unwanted parasite!' cried out Vimla, feeling a lump near her throat as she tried holding back her tears.

'I know what it looks like, but trust me. Things will get better soon.'

'I have been trying to console myself for the past

nine days saying the same thing. Every night before going to bed I think it's going to get better tomorrow. That Tyagiji will come and do right by me. And every day I wake up to have my hopes shattered once again. It's been nine days since I have seen my husband. NINE DAYS! Why hasn't he come to visit me even once? If he doesn't want me to be his wife, he should say so and drop me back to my place!'

Maya tried to console Vimla by holding her hand, but she pulled it back and tucked her hands around her knees which she had folded up, burying her face in it and breaking down into heaving sobs yet again. Vimla had receded into a cold place Maya could not reach into, and although she prodded her to say something the only response she got was a muffled, 'Go tell him I don't want to live here anymore and I want to go home!'

Vimla cried herself to sleep long after Maya had left her, and it was evening by the time she woke up to a knock on her door. She opened her eyes to see who it was, her lids still heavy from all the tears it had shed. Standing at the door she could make out the silhouette of the man her eyes had longed to see for so long. She sprang up on her bed, rubbing her eyes to make sure it was him, and then looked at him again.

'Maya told me you were upset', said Devendra simply, still standing at the doorway, with his hands inside his pockets.

'What else am I supposed to be?' Vimla retorted.

Devendra shrugged slightly, then said with a little more warmth in his voice this time, 'Come with me'. He then turned around and moved out into the balcony, leaning with his arms against the railing and looking down, waiting for Vimla to join him. Vimla got up and walked up to the opposite wall to see herself in the mirror. She looked completely dishevelled; her hair was in a mess, her eyes red and swollen and her lips chapped. She wiped her face with a wet towel, drank some water from the jug which she had in her room and then tied her hair up into a bun before pulling the veil over her head to cover her face, the only time she felt glad she could hide herself behind the veil.

She then stepped outside the door and stood by Devendra's side. Devendra looked at her and opened his mouth to say something but then paused, looked around, and jerked his head to indicate she follow him. He then turned around and walked the length of the balcony, up the staircase and into the terrace, with Vimla keeping at his heels.

Vimla entered the terrace after Devendra and they both walked towards the other end of the roof which overlooked the rest of the village. There were no walls skirting the terrace and if one were not careful, they could fall over the edge. Vimla eyed the edge anxiously as Devendra neared it, but his sure-footed pacing showed that this was obviously not his first time here.

Vimla waited for him to say something as he continued pacing up and down the edge, hands in pocket and head bent low as if deep in thought. He then stopped abruptly and walked right up to where Vimla was standing, slowly lifting her veil up so he could see her straight in the eye as he said, 'I know you are upset because of how you have been treated so far in the house. Maybe you also heard things you did not like. The atmosphere around the house is not right and very disturbed presently. There are a lot of things going on that you don't understand'.

Vimla listened without saying a word. She stood there quietly as Devendra continued, 'You have to understand something today. You will never get anything from this house which brides typically do; no new clothes, jewellery, gifts or even proper love and acceptance of your in-laws. So, you will never come to me with complaints of why you are not being showered with gifts like most newly-weds are by their in-laws'.

At this point Vimla could no longer hold the resentment that had been building up inside her. 'Well, in that case why are you keeping me here? Why don't you send me back to my parents?' she whined, fighting to keep tears from rolling down her eyes. 'And what use are new clothes and jewelleries to me if I am not even being treated with love and respect. Clothes will wear off with time, the sheen of jewelleries will fade too. Relationships are built not over such fleeting objects but with values that stand the test of time; values such as trust, love, and respect, all things that I am yet to see from you or

anyone else here.'

'Yes, you are right. You have been denied even the basic courtesy of being a guest in the house, something which no one deserves, let alone a newly wed bride. But remember something today that I am telling you. You do not have to worry about anything from now on, nor do you have to expect anything from my family.' He then put his hand on her shoulders, pulled her closer and said, 'Because from today, whatever it is that you want, whatever it is your heart desires, *I will fulfil them*. You will turn to no one but me for anything it is you want. *I* will be there for you, today, tomorrow, and for the rest of your life.'

And although there were no walls to echo off around the terrace, Devendra's words reverberated in Vimla's heart and left an indelible mark upon it. The 'I' rung through the vibrations in the air and suddenly lifted the pall of gloom and despair that had been eating Vimla from within for the past nine days. She suddenly felt considerably lighter as she sniffled, 'Ok, I will remember that'.

It was a beautiful evening; the sun had set beyond the horizon and the twilight colours which painted the sky in a deep shade of orange and purple brought out a vibrant hue which Vimla had only now begun to appreciate. She felt as though for the past nine days, the veil was not just covering her head but also filtering out the colours from her life, and now that she had it lifted off from her

head she could enjoy once again the world in all its colourful glory.

Devendra and Vimla stood side by side, shoulders brushing lightly, as they both gazed up at the sky where the first stars had started coming out. Slowly and ever so gently Devendra lifted his arm and put it around Vimla's shoulder; she shuddered slightly under the touch of his hand and, her eyes not breaking away from the beauty of the night sky, smiled from her heart for the first time since coming to Khilwai. This moment right here was nowhere near the ones Vimla had imagined married life to be like, but it was everything she had hoped it would be.

VIMLA, ON THE CREST OF DOUBT

THE NEXT DAY Devendra had to leave for Lucknow to attend to his work and he came to see Vimla one more time before leaving.

'I have taken a longer leave than I had thought I would. There were too many things for me to take care of here at home. But now I have to go back to work and so I'm leaving for Lucknow today', he said.

Vimla looked slightly taken aback by the news, for it was only yesterday that she had thought they would now be able to spend more time together and everything would become as she had hoped it would. Seeing the look on Vimla's face, Devendra said, 'Don't worry, I have asked *bhaiya* to drop you to your house. He will go with you to Kanpur where you will stay till I am able to bring you to live with me'.

'Oh, okay. If that's what you say', came a meek reply.

'I will be writing to you from Lucknow. We will stay in touch until the next time we see each other.'

'I will look forward to your letter.'

'And remember what I had told you yesterday. Always keep that in mind.'

'Yes, I remember.'

Beaming at her, Devendra then bid a final goodbye to his wife and was soon on his way to Lucknow.

Vimla spent two days in Khilwai after Devendra's departure during which time she faced further heat from some of the members of his family, his uncle being one of them. However, remembering Devendra's promise, Vimla wore her veil like a shield behind which she kept herself as far removed as possible from all the bitterness she faced. She mostly confined herself to her room save for a few brief escapes into the terrace, where she sat by herself reminiscing the lingering feeling of the only happy memory she had with Devendra, and wondering when again she would be united with her husband.

Early in the morning on the third day since Devendra had left for Lucknow, his elder brother Satbir came to see Vimla and told her to pack her luggage and come with him, that he was to take her back home, to her parents. Vimla, who on Devendra's word had been expecting him to take her home sooner, was nevertheless glad that she was finally going back.

She packed a few of her clothes and some other essential articles in a small suitcase, locked the rest of her possessions in the large trunk she had brought with herself from Kanpur, and then proceeded to meet her brother-in-law downstairs. He was waiting for her, along with a young boy named Shankar, who was their household help. The boy rushed to take the suitcase from Vimla's hands as soon as she emerged from the stairwell, and the three then exited the house to get into a rickshaw which had been called to take them to the railway station.

No one from the family had come out to meet Vimla before she left except for Maya, who stood by the door waving limply at her as the rickshaw pulled away from the house. The smell of dirt which rose from under the wheels of the rickshaw filled Vimla's nostrils up as it made its way through the unpaved village roads towards the railway station, and she felt her cheek muscles stretch from end to end as Vimla caught herself smiling smugly under her veil. Home was calling, and Vimla had never been more eager to answer its call.

It was late in the evening when Vimla and her escorts, Satbir and Shankar, arrived at her home. The journey from Kanpur railway station to her house was such a ride of emotions as Vimla had never expected or experienced before. She felt a peculiar mix of elation and relief surging through her body with every tree, every park, every lane and every shop they crossed – and as the familiarity of the scenes increased the nearer they got to her home

she felt her emotions almost escaping her body. She suddenly had a strong urge to jump out of the rickshaw and touch the ground to feel the grains of sand in her hands; she had never felt as closely tied to the city she grew up in as she did now.

When the rickshaw finally pulled up in front of the gates of her house, Vimla took a deep breath before getting down. She stood there momentarily in front of the house, her eyes scouring over its outline she so distinctly remembered, and yet it felt as though everything about it had changed now that she was married. She then saw the front door open and out came her mother, walking hesitantly at first but then quickening her steps to welcome them as soon as she recognised who they were. Rani stepped outside the gate and even before the two could exchange any words, she locked her daughter in an embrace so tight that only now Vimla realised the full weight of the absence her mother had left in her life.

When they finally broke away from the hug, Rani said, 'Why didn't you write to me beforehand of your arrival? I would have made some special snacks for you all'. She then looked over Vimla's shoulder and asked, 'Is Devendra also here?'

'No, he had to go back to Lucknow for his work. I came here instead with my *jethji*.'

'Of course, of course', said Rani and then stepped forward to greet Satbir, who was still sitting in the rickshaw. 'I hope you had a pleasant journey.

Please come inside, I'll have some refreshments prepared for you', she said to him cordially, a wide smile etched on her face.

'No need to bother with that', Satbir replied curtly. 'I just came to drop Vimla off. I will be leaving now.' He looked at the manservant, who then immediately got off the rickshaw and carried Vimla's suitcase to her front door.

'What? No! No! You cannot leave like this', said Rani, a little stunned. 'It's your first time at our house. How can we let you leave empty handed? Please come inside for at least a cup of tea.'

'I cannot. I have a train to catch', Satbir grunted. By this time, Shankar had returned from dropping off Vimla's suitcase at the door and was now sitting next to Satbir, who then said flatly to the rickshaw puller, 'Take us back to the station'. And before Rani could add any further words of protest, the rickshaw puller turned around and tugged the duo back the same way they had come. The abrupt departure sent a clear signal to Vimla's family.

The look of shock registered on Rani's face made Vimla feel bad for her mother, and she took herself by surprise when the words that came out of her mouth were, 'Don't worry ma, everything is fine. Jethji really had to go back in a hurry because he had some urgent business to attend to at home. It was because of it that he was a little tensed and so spoke that way to you'.

Somewhat reassured, Rani smiled warmly at

her daughter as she placed a hand on her cheek. 'I'm so glad to see you. Come, let's go inside. I'll make your favourite carrot *halwa* which should go well with all the spicy gossips I'm sure you have about your in-laws to share with me.'

Vimla hesitated for a second and then said, 'Well, not so much. I had a wonderful time there. They were treating me like a princess'. Vimla now began to build her glass house.

It was not like Vimla to deliberately try and hide something from her mother, but she felt compelled to present her in-laws in a good light – for it somehow felt like her own fault if she didn't. Rani's face lit up when she heard this and the two women gleefully made their way into the house, holding each other by the waist and talking about things that mattered to no one in the world but them.

Vimla's return home brought a spark back into the house which, without her, had sunk into a monotone of wonton routines. Now she was the only outlier in the otherwise well-oiled cogs of the Shastri family and her presence had brought back the disruption Rani, and even Shastri, had sorely missed. After Vimla's bidai, the house had started feeling empty, which also had to do with the fact that Dinesh had now shifted to London after his visa got approved where he took up his practice as a surgeon, and that Indu and Manju had gone back to their respective homes after Vimla's bidai. So, where once it had been difficult for all members

of the Shastri family to fit comfortably under one roof, Ramesh, Rani and their two sons Umesh and Rakesh now had all the rooms in the house to themselves but no way to compensate for the empty spaces left behind.

Vimla, for her part, felt the need to carry on with the charade she had so unthinkingly started, and spent long hours with her mother telling her stories about her in-laws; stories of how fresh the food was in the village coming straight from the farm, of how they added ghee to everything making them taste so good, of how beautiful it was to go out in the evenings for a walk down the lane, how amiable her sisters-in-law were and how peaceful it was there in her new home for no one seemed to be bothered with books or studying. Vimla said them with so much conviction that she herself started believing those stories, even if it was only a part of her that had lived them out.

On her second day in Kanpur, Vimla received a letter that was addressed to her. It was a letter from Devendra. This was the first time in her life Vimla had received any form of letter from anyone, and she was very excited to see her name written across the face of the envelope. "*Vimla Tyagi*". She held the letter close to her heart and went straight to her room where she tucked herself in her bed and then opened the envelope ever so delicately to take the letter out. Holding it in her hands which were trembling slightly, Vimla began reading the letter,

her heart pounding against the pillow on top of which she lay with every word she read; words that seemed to have been written from worlds away and yet felt closer than the sound of her own breath.

She read the letter, cover to cover, three times before putting it down. Her heart swooned over the contents of the letter and she lay in the bed with it clutched in her hand, thinking about how nobody had ever talked as nicely to her in person as Devendra did over this piece of parchment. Giggling to herself, she then folded the letter, got out of her bed and carefully placed it inside her suitcase in between one of her sarees.

Then she walked across the room to her cupboard where she rummaged through her old school stuff to find a notebook and a pen. Vimla then sat down on the floor and began writing back to Devendra with an unwavering purpose and desire that had never been channelled through the pen she now wielded in all her years of writing letters or essays for school literature. Her hand flowed over the paper to string together every alphabet, every syllable as carefully and tastefully as beads of pearls in a necklace, and when she was finally done with it, she ran her fingers across the letter and saw it for what it was; her heart poured out in ink.

Here began Vimla's lifelong tryst with letters, words, sentences, her words flowing into bits of notebook paper, drawing images for every reader who reads them, bringing alive nuances, creating

ambiences that left indelible impressions.

And thus, also began a long, elaborate and arduous exchange of letters between Devendra and Vimla, for the joy his letters brought was in equal measure to the disheartening reminder of their living apart. Still, Vimla waited with bated breath everyday to hear the sound of the postman's arrival, the high pitch ring of his approaching bicycle met with her elevated pulse as she would take the letter from him and rush back inside to read it in her room's privacy. Vimla would read Devendra's letters in a hurry, impatient to reach to the bottom which was always signed as, '*Yours, Devendra*'. Her heart never failed to skip a beat whenever she read those last two words; two words around which she had started building her entire world. But even though she would read his letters fast, her replies to them were written with utmost diligence and patience, often drawing heavily from the artful dialogues of Hindi songs and cinemas which Vimla was so strongly connected to.

However, while such a back and forth of correspondence between Vimla and Devendra had started becoming an integral part of her life, another letter which was addressed to her father Ramesh Shastri had dropped like a bomb in the Shastri household and was giving Rani and her husband sleepless nights, unbeknownst to Vimla. A week after Vimla's return to Kanpur, Shastri had received a letter from Devendra's father, Raghubir

Singh, and when he first read its contents it pulled the rug from under his feet.

In the letter, Singh said that his niece was going to get married in a week's time, but there would be no need for them to send Vimla back for the wedding because, after consulting with his brother, they had decided to break all ties with the Shastri family. They were looking for another woman for his son and they would get Devendra married alongside his niece's wedding ceremony. It further said that they felt deceived and disrespected by the lack of 'hospitality and generosity' shown towards them by Shastri and so felt it in their best interests to sever all relations with them.

Daughters in an Indian family are typically raised with the idea and sole purpose of one day getting them married and sending them off to another house, and thus the perception of the girl being the responsibility of the parents to being the responsibility of her husband and in-laws is formed. This inevitably gives rise to a skewered power balance in a patriarchal society which is emblematic of the importance laid down on the groom over the bride. And so, if a father intends to give his daughter's hand in marriage, he must do so along with a sum of money that compensates for his daughter being just that, a daughter.

In India therefore, dowry is an unsaid and oftentimes explicitly asked for demand from the groom's family which the bride's family must

submissively acquiesce to. In Vimla's case, Singh had expected to receive a good sum of money as dowry for Devendra since not only was he well educated, but he also held a government job which, in dowry-negotiating terms, meant he was a prime candidate in the marriage market.

This expectation was also fuelled by Singh's brother, who had a daughter of his own around the same age as Vimla, and who he intended to get married off, and so in typical what-goes-around-comes-around fashion, had to save money as dowry for her marriage. Singh's brother had hoped to use a portion of money which Devendra's dowry would fetch to use as dowry for his own daughter's wedding.

However, while Shastri had saved up a considerable sum to give as *kanyadaan* upon Vimla's marriage, they had to spend that money on Dinesh's ticket and visa for London, since as far as priority went, it was more important that Dinesh continued climbing up his career ladder than to give that money away as dowry. Although there had been serious contemplation on this issue between Dinesh and his father in private, they had ultimately decided that perhaps dowry would not be such a major issue when it came to Vimla's marriage, and this money would be better utilised in advancing Dinesh's career pursuits.

But this did not sit well with Devendra's family members who had taken a personal affront to the fact that their son had not fetched any dowry, a sign

of utter disrespect that could not go unanswered. The cold indifference Vimla was subjected to during her time in Khilwai was a result of this perceived personal attack on their ego, and the letter received by Shastri informing him of their intention to sever all relations was the ultimate flexing of it.

Vimla, however, went about her days unfazed by all that was happening around her like a living personification of the old adage 'ignorance is bliss'. Her new world was now constructed around the letters she exchanged with Devendra, and he was helping her build this world with rose coloured glasses, since in none of the letters did he bring up news of any such trouble brewing at his home. Although Vimla did find it a bit odd when in one of the letters Devendra mentioned about his cousin's (his uncle's daughter) wedding but said there would be no need for her to come and that he would attend it alone. She thought it was odd because as a sister-in-law, she felt she should be as involved in the wedding as anybody else in the family, but when she tried insisting that she should accompany him in her reply to his letter, she was reassured by Devendra that everything was fine and he asked her to stay back at home.

And so it happened that while Devendra went to Khilwai to attend the wedding, Vimla continued to stay back in Kanpur in oblivious peace and tranquility. On the other end of the spectrum, Rani was worrying herself sick over the fact that

her daughter's marital home had been ruined even before it could begin and Shastri spent hours sitting quietly in the living room and mulling over his daughter's future. However, this was not the end of Vimla's story as fate intended, and over the next couple of days more drama began to unfold.

Shastri received another letter in his name from Devendra's father and this time there was none of the harsh words and tone previously used in the first letter, but rather a solemn and politely written letter which informed of Singh's father's sudden demise, along with a request to send Vimla back to Khilwai where she belonged since it was her home.

'Oh, *now* he wants me to send my daughter over to his house', was Shastri's first reaction when he read the letter and told Rani about it. 'He wanted nothing to do with my daughter in times of celebrations, but now when there has been a death in the family, he expects me to forget everything and send Vimla back? They can very well rot in there, for I am not going to send my daughter back!'

But Shastri's fuming indignation was met with Rani's adamant and headstrong stance that Vimla now belonged to her new home and it is not becoming of a woman to stay with her parents even after her marriage. It came to the point where Rani literally broke down in tears before Shastri let his stoic guard down and agreed to sending Vimla back to Khilwai to her in-laws' house.

Rani broke the news of baba's death to Vimla

the next day and then told her that she had been asked to go back to her home in Khilwai, and so she should start making arrangements for her travel. The very same afternoon Shankar, the manservant who had accompanied Vimla from Khilwai to Kanpur, came with a letter for her from Devendra detailing the passing away of his grandfather and asking her to come to Khilwai. Shankar had personally come to deliver the letter so that she could return back with him and would not have to travel alone from Kanpur. And so, in the space of a single abrupt day, from sitting idly in her home and wondering how and when she would next see Devendra, Vimla found herself on a train that night taking her back to her new home but under circumstances very different from what she had imagined.

Vimla reached Khilwai early next morning. Her head was completely blank of thoughts as she neared her in-laws' house – for this was unchartered territory for Vimla; she had never faced death in her family in her lifetime. Vimla had no clue as to what was deemed appropriate behaviour at a time like this and that too so early in her marriage, and as soon as she entered her house and saw her in-laws huddled around the courtyard quietly grieving the death of baba, the first words that instinctively came out of her mouth were, 'So is this how it's going to be now? Am I only going to be called when there has been a death in the family?'

All heads turned in unison at the source of sound to see who it was that spoke so brazenly of death, and yet Vimla's voice was so unoffending and honest that it helped slightly break the atmosphere that had grown tense and morbid. Vimla, however, grew a little anxious when she did not spot Devendra and realised that the men must still be in the gher, and it was only the women who were present in the house. She let out an internal sigh of relief when she saw a welcoming smile on her mother-in-law's face as she got up and walked towards her to greet her. Vimla pulled the veil over her head further down her face as she bent down to touch her mother-in-law's feet, who then gently pulled Vimla up by her shoulders and said, 'Welcome back home, my child'.

Vimla felt a heavy weight lift off her heart upon hearing the words spoken by her mother-in-law, and no sooner had she taken another step into the house, a second woman tottered up to Vimla and wrapped her in her arms. She was her father-in-law's sister, Devki; baba's daughter. With a tear running down her cheek, she looked at Vimla and said, 'It was your name baba had on his lips before he breathed his last'. She placed her hand on Vimla's cheek and sniffled, 'He felt terrible about the way you were treated. Oh, how he longed to see you come back to this house!'

Vimla's return to her marital home was turning out to be a much better experience than she had

hoped for. The cold hearts which Vimla had faced earlier were now warming up to her, and everyone from her mother-in-law and father-in-law to all her other extended in-laws spoke to her in a much more friendly manner. Although the demeanour of a few of them was somewhat lacking in genuine warmth, they all nevertheless welcomed her back into the house as one of their own. And while the disingenuous pleasantries might have been too much for Vimla's guileless brain to fathom amidst all the confusing and obscure ways in which human emotions function, she was pleasantly surprised in finding an unexpected friend in Devki who seemed to have developed a special bond with Vimla. Given how separated the living arrangements were for men and women in the village, Vimla had had hardly any time alone with Devendra since her coming to Khilwai, and it was Devki who kept Vimla company most of her time there.

Devki and Vimla became really close in the few days she was in Khilwai, and it was through her that Vimla came to know of the many things that transpired behind her back while she was in Kanpur. Although Vimla was not told about the letter and her in-laws' intentions to remarry Devendra to another woman, she learned about the dowry, or lack thereof which had been the root cause of all the hard times Vimla had to endure when she had come here after the marriage.

'But what changed then? Why is everyone so

nice to me suddenly? My father hasn't paid them any dowry still, or has he?' Vimla asked, confused.

'It's because of baba. He reminded us that never in our family have we deserted any of our daughters-in-law right after the marriage. He kept insisting that we bring you back. Even until his final moments, he kept saying it would be a grave sin and he would not be able to face God if we turned our back on you like this', Devki replied solemnly.

She continued with a heavy voice, 'You know, he really couldn't believe that we weren't inviting you for Mithlesh's wedding. On the night of the wedding, as we all were saying our final goodbyes at the time of her bidai, I still remember the look in baba's eyes – sad, pathetic and helpless. My father was a bold and fierce man, and I had never seen a look of such defeat in his eyes as I saw then'. Devki paused for a second to catch a lump in her throat, and then said, 'Later that night he breathed his last, but not before he told bhaiya one last time to bring you back to our home'.

Devki told her how, after baba's death, even the people in the village had started talking amongst themselves and asking uncomfortable questions about her whereabouts and why she hadn't come for Mithlesh's wedding; some even saying that it was because they had turned Vimla away that baba had died.

There are few forces of nature stronger than social stigma which compels a man to act in a

certain way. Whether it was regret and remorse from how his father had passed away or the way his neighbours had started whispering about it, something had stoked in Singh's heart that made him immediately send for Vimla to come back to his house. What baba was not able to convince his son to do in his life, he was able to persuade him to do so in his death. It really was surreal, thought Vimla, the way her fortunes had turned on the back of an old man's death.

Vimla's second coming to Khilwai was short and uneventful as compared to the first time she had come here. Although she had no real or meaningful interactions other than with Devki while she was here, she still managed to have a few sweet conversations with her mother-in-law Lajjawati and established amicable relations with her other sisters-in-law, which was a lot more than could be said for her when she had come here after marriage. She had only been here four days when Devendra told her they would be leaving together the next day, that she should have her luggage packed and ready, and that he had already written to her father about their travel plans ahead of their journey.

The following day, as the first sign of light crept into the courtyard, Vimla and Devendra bid farewell to their family members after which they both got into a rickshaw to take them to the railway station. The train journey back to Kanpur was one of the most memorable Vimla had ever taken. It

was a journey not just of the two bodies from one place to another, but also of two hearts and two souls on a journey of discovering one another. Even though they had exchanged countless letters, she and Devendra still found each other lost in conversations about everything under the sun.

While talking about the different circumstances of their upbringing, Devendra said to Vimla, 'You know, my father is a *daaroga* while yours is a professor. So there is obviously going to be a difference in the way they think and act. Some people hold on to rituals and traditions very strongly while others are able to think past it. So you must not take to heart the words of old men, for they are set in their ways and it is really difficult to reason with them'.

Vimla looked at him and could see a hint of pain and guilt in his eyes. She replied softly, 'Yes, I know and I understand. After all, rituals and traditions are there for a reason'.

'Yes, that is true. But tell me one thing, how was my parents' behaviour towards you once I left for Lucknow the last time you were in Khilwai?'

Vimla was a little taken aback by this question. She thought Devendra was still somewhat weighed down by guilt for how she had felt on her first visit to Khilwai and wanted him to stop feeling that way. Hoping that he would put this matter to rest she said, 'There is no scale in the world that can accurately weigh and measure the behaviour of our

parents towards us. It is not for us to ponder upon the meaning of their actions, but only trust in the fact that whatever they do, they do it in our best interests'.

Vimla's reply was met with a long silence by Devendra, filled only by the rhythmic chugging of the train.

Vimla waited for him to say something, but Devendra did not break the silence and instead turned his gaze outside the window. It was as if what she said had warranted not a reply but reflection, which is what he did by looking out of the window at nothing in particular. She looked at her husband sitting opposite her on the train berth, watching the landscape passing them by in a blur of different colours, and in that moment she felt herself wanting for nothing more in life, completely content with what she had.

The day stretched into night and as the train pulled up at Kanpur railway station, Vimla felt a wrenching feeling in her gut as she realised they were about to part once again. The train's sluggish entry into the platform and its eventual halt felt all too soon for Vimla. She wished she could have continued on the train journey with Devendra till Lucknow, or any other place for it really was not about the destination. But the figure of her father standing on the platform was a bitter reminder that this indeed was her stop, and she had to get down here. Devendra helped her with her suitcase as the two stepped outside the train to meet and greet

Shastri. Devendra had time only to exchange a few formal pleasantries with his father-in-law before he had to board the train again.

With Shastri present, Devendra and Vimla could only express with their eyes the agony of separation they both felt.

Devendra stood at the door and waved at Vimla as the train started pulling away from the platform and slowly gathered speed. Vimla was rooted at the spot, her hand held up waving until the train became a dot and then disappeared into the horizon. It was only when her father nudged her that she turned around and started walking with him towards the station's exit.

Devendra and Vimla were heading in two different directions now, but the journey on which they had embarked upon together from Khilwai had brought their hearts beating together and going in the same direction now for the rest of their lives.

VIMLA, THE HOMEMAKER

THERE WAS A new person in Vimla's life now.

So long, life had been all about herself. Vimla surrounded by her parents, siblings, friends. Now there was a man, someone she did not yet know well, but someone who had made her his own. Someone, she had accepted as her own. Who was he? What kind of a man was he? Her sisters acknowledged he was young and handsome. Beyond that…?

Devendra of Village Khilwai

Devendra's life had started in the daaroga's grand house in village Khilwai, in Garh Mukteshwar tehsil of Ghaziabad district in Uttar Pradesh. Garh Mukteshwar is said to be part of the ancient Hastinapur kingdom and mentioned in the *Bhagavat Purana*. Today it is a pilgrim town where the river Ganges is worshipped in its many temples. In the 1970s, Khilwai had a few hundred households, basically of agrarian communities.

A local priest claimed that they had records of the Tyagi family tree for 20 generations and Devendra belonged to the 16th generation. He had studied in the village school till 5th standard. It is only after that, that Devendra had left the village to go to middle and high school, like most children in Khilwai village did.

A Village Pradhan, who had been a childhood friend, recalled that as a child, Devendra had been a very simple boy who used to be engrossed in his own world; most times, he would roam around in the neighbourhood farms or be busy playing. The family was affluent and he was a very loved child.

He was very good in kabaddi. Tall, agile, and light on his feet, he was quick on the ground and would play kabaddi very well, would never get caught. 'Our mohalla was called Neemwaala Mohalla, because in our locality, there was the oldest and only neem tree then. There was no other neem tree in our village at the time and so our area was called neemwaala mohalla. In our neemwaala mohalla, Devendra was such a good kabaddi player that our neemwaala mohalla would be on one side, and the entire village would be on the other side', the friend said.

'After he left the village to study further, our contact became less frequent', the friend said, recalling that Devendra had always loved being involved in farming and agriculture and took deep interest in it from early childhood.

He never fought with anyone, even when other children would fight he would never get into a fight with anyone. Since his childhood he had always been in good terms with everyone, there would be no one who could hold a grudge against him or hated him, a trait which he carried with himself in his adult life as well. Harijans used to live in his neighbourhood, and even with them he would be very well behaved. His humility and good nature was his defining characteristic. No one had any grudge against him because he never gave anyone any reason to.

He was such a person that he didn't even accept dowry when he got married, even though it resulted in many older members of his family to throw an anger tantrum, the villagers recalled.

Devendra would come to the village sometime during Holi, Diwali etc., and would always meet and greet everyone with utmost love and respect. He was very well behaved. He knew a lot about agriculture. Gave many insightful suggestions to improve yield and production, many of his farmer acquaintances in the ancestral village later recalled.

Humility was the greatest aspect of his character, he would never treat anyone beneath him, he would treat everyone with respect, and was loved by everyone.

'People in the village hardly knew what he was doing in his professional life.' He would meet everyone, greet them, *aur bhai kya chal raha hai,*

batao chacha, would enter other people's houses and meet and greet them... *aise hi ghar me ghus jaana*... although he never constructed anything, school or road or anything permanent in the village, but still he resided in everyone's heart.'

Lucknow

The first few years of married life were full of romantic indulgences. Vimla went with the flow and became completely smitten with her marriage.

Devendra was in Literacy House in Lucknow, as a research fellow. He was working towards education, understanding education policy.*

As Lucknow and Kanpur were not too far from each other, now began not only the almost daily exchange of letters but short visits from Devendra.

He came several times to Kanpur to see Vimla and plead with his mother-in-law to send her with him to Lucknow. She was old-fashioned, and would not let her go before her 'gauna', ritual of consummation of marriage, which began with child marriage in India. Vimla and Devendra were two young adults wanting to be with eachother and no amount of incomplete rituals could keep them apart.

After his fourth visit to Kanpur, Vimla's mother finally relented and let her go to her husband in

* (http://indialiteracyboard.org/about-us.php)

Lucknow. In the late 1960s, Lucknow was a bustling city, with the flavour of the 18th century lingering, yet a city moving towards becoming the State capital. Life enthralled her. Vimla lived with Devendra, in a tiny house and went about sightseeing eagerly. Devendra and his friends accompanied her, showing her the city. They went for long walks, her first visit to a restaurant, a photo studio where they posed for half-a-dozen beautiful pictures that still hang on her walls, keeping the memories of those days fresh.

Vimla reminiscences, 'I was not very good at studies, but was very good at practical work. I used to write so well in Hindi, the articulation and words expressed were beautiful, the letters I used to write for him are evidence'.

Once she asked him, what was it about her that he liked so much? 'See', Devendra said, 'first of all I really liked the environment you were brought up in. Everyone was about studies, education was given so much importance, I wanted to be a part of such an environment. Your brothers are so well educated, your father is a scholar, what else do I want'.

After that he had added philosophically, 'If I earn even 1 rupee, I know you know its value. I am sure of the values you must have been brought up with'.

The sojourn in Lucknow was sweet and short, heralding the arrival of Prerna, their daughter. For Devendra, her care at this sensitive juncture became

important, so he took her to Moradabad, where his elder brother and his family lived. His brother was a PAC (Provincial Armed Constabulary) official and had adequate accommodation and facilities.

A pregnant Vimla also took another unusual and bold step in life. She began studying in order to give the intermediate class examination. She felt, her brothers and sisters were all highly educated, and so was her husband. Her marital family too wanted her to complete schooling, so she decided to appear for Class 12 exam through a private board. Thus, for almost a year, she lived in Moradabad, mostly spending her time, studying. 'My *devar* would take me to give my exams. And I cleared my exam that year', Vimla recalls proudly.

Devendra's mother also came from the village to take care of Vimla. For some reason, Vimla's sister-in-law was not very warm towards her, She was indifferent and often rude, and did not pay any heed to what Vimla said or wanted.

At the time there were too many people living in the house in Moradabad: Devendra's brother and wife and their children, a younger brother and Vimla. Then there were the children of Devendra's uncle, they had come to Moradabad for studying.

'Later, my mother in-law took me to the village to spend the remaining days of the pregnancy in the village itself.' For Vimla, after Kanpur and Lucknow, Moradabad was a prison. Even the village was better.

Vimla was good at practical things. She would

write very good letters to Devendra. 'He would be stunned at how I would write. He would say he sometimes would be embarrassed as he didn't know how to reply properly to the kind of letters I wrote', Vimla remembers.

Devendra used to write frequently before this. As Vimla felt suffocated inside the house all the time, she would write to him to come take her away from the village. Vimla would even write to her father, asking to be taken back to Kanpur, but he too paid no heed to Vimla's requests.

Before getting married, Devendra had taken the job in Lucknow, because it was recommended by someone called Vyasji, who he revered. The work did not satisfy Devendra, however. This Vyasji was posted in Gujarat. Devendra finally called Vyasji and told him about his dissatisfaction with the Lucknow job, and that he wanted to leave. But Vyas told him to hold out a bit, as he was soon expecting a vacancy in the Agro-Economic Research Centre in Vallabh Vidyanagar, for the post of Joint Director. And so, because Vyas had told him to, Devendra continued working at the Literacy Department. He used to say that 'there is no real work here, I won't even be able to write and do my academic researches here like this'. Then, after some time, a post opened and Devendra got into a research job. Vimla was expecting her first child, when he got the offer from Gujarat, Vallabh Vidyanagar. Vimla was with his family in his village.

After moving to his new job, Devendra tried

getting Vimla to Gujarat. He wrote to his father asking for permission, but Raghubir scolded his son, saying Vimla was in no condition to travel, she should be staying home – 'with all of us', he emphasised. 'She is not a roti-making machine' Vimla's angry father-in-law added. Devendra then requested his father to let Vimla be taken to Moradabad for checkups.

For those seven months of pregnancy, Vimla would be taken to Moradabad periodically for medical checkups, in government hospitals where free check-ups were available. When she was past eighth month, the last one-and-a-half months, Vimla again spent in Moradabad. Vimla's first child was born in the middle of the night, at 2.30 am and the PAC delivery room had to be especially opened as the jawans carried her in to give birth to her first born, a bonny baby girl.

Vimla was in Moradabad for about a month after the birth and then came to Khilwai, where again Vimla stayed for a month. Finally, Devendra came to the village to take his wife and 2-month old daughter to Gujarat. Vimla's heart sang, '*Dukh bhare din bitey bhai...Sukh bhare din ayo re!*'

Gujarat

It was domesticity in full bloom, like an enchanting dreamflower, that enveloped Vimla for the next ten years. In Gujarat, she spent four years, giving birth to her son Prashant, with a miscarriage in between and raising her young family. For a while, all her other interests were subsumed.

Devendra never made her feel any less because of her lack of education. He let her be her way, the way she was, carefree and not being prone to getting worried.

They had a very happy and contented life together. But even he failed to encourage her to pursue her interest in dancing. She was passionately engrossed in her husband to chase her personal passion and a career in dancing. Her family life was what became central for her.

Vimla would also watch a lot of movies as a child, and in the movies, the love scenes would just be shown as two flowers meeting, and then there would be a baby. And then, this baby too would grow up quickly to become a full grown star, Rajendra Kumar in *Mother India*. But when it happened to her, when she had a baby, Vimla would think 'why are they not growing at all, why are they still so small?'

She would say this to Devendra and he would joke, 'you hold her from one side, I will from the other and pull at her, then she will grow faster'.

'I wanted the children to grow fast so that I could be free and learn dancing and everything', Vimla says.

'This is a kind of dance that you are doing', Devendra would respond, running after them, picking up their stuff (shoes, toys). He would joke:

'Aise hi to karte hai dance, jaise tum kar rahi ho.'

Vimla had a sister who was very good at singing, and she would also play different instruments like Dholak and Sitar. Vimla was very good at dance. So, as children, the two formed a very good pair together. 'We used to practice together as well. After watching Vyjayanthimala's movies, I would lock myself in my room and practice her steps in front of the mirror', Vimla recalls. However, the two sisters had never got any real encouragement from anyone in their own house or later, to pursue this side of their talent.

Though, Vimla did not go back to her dancing later in life, she always wanted that one of her children should learn dancing.

Their brothers were doctors, DC Tyagi and UC Tyagi... these were achievements to be proud of. 'That is why, when I told my husband my brothers prefix their name with 'Dr' and you write just Mr DS Tyagi, he paid heed to what I said', Vimla says. That's when he went ahead and did his PhD, and got his doctorate and he too became Dr DS Tyagi, Vimla adds.

Vimla had once said to Devendra: 'If you want to do a PhD and you don't have the money to support our family, don't worry, there's no need for you to ask for money from your house, your father. You can sell my bangles and do it.' Thus Vimla had also offered to let go of her bangles, her precious *kangans*, often an Indian woman's only

asset, and this showed how keen she was that her husband should be also a doctorate and acquire the distinction to be called 'Dr Tyagi'. Devendra was very proud of her, and loved her for how selfless she was.

The couple lived in a small flat inside Vallabh Vidyanagar in Ahmedabad. They slept on an iron bed. There were two rooms in the small house and a kitchen. Vimla would have to walk long distances to throw the garbage. She learned to do most of the household work there, they had no household help. 'So, I did everything myself', says Vimla.

'Once I asked him to buy some furniture and curtains for the house. He very calmly said, "listen, I don't want to stay fixed in one place. You keep talking about sofa, curtains, but understand that I am like a bird, I want to fly, be everywhere."'

'That is when, with a hint of agitation, he told me, "Yes, today you tell me and write down everything you want, curtains and all". The next day, when we got new curtains, he said, "now, do you want to sit here only for the rest of your life? You might as well settle in a village then. You can sit comfortably over there for the rest of your life"', Vimla recalls.

'Hey, but it's your friends only that keep coming to the house, don't you want them to sit comfortably?'

'What... what about my friends? I can put a cloth over a trunk and making it into a table, job done. What else do you need?'

'Oh, come on, you are at such a high position.'

'Oh shut up.'

'And then he took my dupatta and put it over a chest, and said, "see, now it's a table."'

'Oye, that's my dupatta!'

'So what!'

'In Gujarat, at the beginning, we had nothing but a trunk in our room. So, he took my dupatta and put it over it to make it into a table because Vyasji was supposed to be coming.'

'Oho, it's such a small makeshift table, how will you place the tea cups on it?'

'We will hold it in our hands! You go look after the children now, and stop worrying about this.'

'I was also from not a very affluent family but had strong values. He had made me promise in the beginning, not to ask for material things from him. But what could I ask from a man who himself makes a trunk into a table?'

'My clothes used to be a little shabby', Vimla admits. Once when Prem had come to visit them, she was washing clothes, and her sister must have noticed something. She said to her brother-in-law, 'at least buy her some new sweaters'.

'You are a heroine, you are a heroine, she talks a lot about you, praises you', was Devendra's reply. Prem was the owner of two large estates.

In Gujarat, Devendra and Vimla's beautiful relationship was appreciated by friends and family. Devendra was a tease, he would tease Vimla a lot.

'Vyasji, Jodha sahab, and we were all neighbours in Gujarat. I became very good friends with Mrs Vyas. I met her at the milk store first, where we were both standing in queue to get milk. Prerna was a baby then, about 2-3 months old. I had Prerna with me at the time I was standing in the queue, and she was crying a lot. Mrs Vyas intervened and asked, what happened, why is she crying so much? I said, "the baby has rashes on her back, that's why she is crying.' The lady then invited me over to her house, saying, "come with me."'

She said, 'I'll apply an ointment which will give her a lot of relief'. She took the milk pouch from me and escorted me to her home.

While getting in, Vimla saw the name plate on the door which read, 'Dr V Vyas', and she was intrigued. She remembered Bhaisaab (Vimla called her husband Bhaisaab) kept mentioning 'Vyasji, Vyasji' a lot, 'so I assumed him to be some hotshot'.

And then, there was this woman who looked simple in appearance, 'and was carrying my milk for me and leading me into his house, so I thought who is this woman entering this house like this, maybe some servant or someone. She then took hold of the baby and applied some home-made ointment which was prepared by crushing some medicinal leaves together to the rash. It immediately had a soothing effect on the baby, and Prerna stopped crying and soon fell asleep'.

The lady then started asking Vimla about

herself: who she was and when had she come to this part of the town, where did she come from etc. 'When I told her my husband, Devendra Tyagi, was here and I came along with him, she immediately recognised the name. She must have heard Vyas mention his name as well.'

She then said, 'Oh, so you are Devendra's wife'.

'But I never mentioned or suggested that she must be Vyasji's wife', Vimla recalls, because she had seen him before, and he was a very handsome man. 'But I hadn't met his wife before, so didn't know who she was. Vyasji would always look smart, with a suit and a tie and everything. His wife, on the other hand, wore a plain and simple saree, and had a a very simple and plain appearance. But then she introduced herself as Mrs Vyas.'

Afterwards, Vimla and Mrs Vyas became very close and good friends.

Devendra first worked under Vyasji as a research student. Later he was a PhD student. Prashant happened in Gujarat, nearly two years after Prerna.

'I used to have a lot of milk from Amul dairy in Gujarat. During Prashant's time I had a lot of milk to feed him.' Devendra would joke, 'see this is nice, you're in Gandhiji's home State'.

'I would say, we get a lot of things to eat and drink.'

Devendra had a habit of always having people over at the house. The house they stayed in was so small, she would wonder how he could bring so many people over.

Plus, then Vimla would have to make food for everyone. Vyasji, Mishraji, Jodha sahab, they would all come. Devendra could not stay without his friends.

By this time, Devendra had begun to travel abroad as a senior government official. Vimla, with small children, was reluctant to travel. To make her respond and agree to go with him, Devendra would joke with Vimla and suggest he had international mistresses. 'I am going to Germany. After all, I have to look after the poor girl over there, make sure she is comfortable. Oh yes, I have a missus in Italy too. See I have a house there as well, and I have another house there too. So, what else do you think, I won't have, you make such tasteless food. I want to live like a king.' He would say such things. These things between husband and wife kept the relationship alive.

How time passes in the journey of life, Vimla now says. Prashant was born in Gujarat in 1970.

VIMLA ON FOREIGN SHORES

AFTER LIVING IN Gujarat for about four years, the Tyagi family came to live in Delhi. They lived in a small rented apartment in the Green Park area of the city, where they stayed for a year.

Devendra, always professionally ambitious, had found a job in the State Trading Corporation in Delhi. This is when Devendra became more focussed on his career and concentrated less on what went on in his home. He was confident that Vimla would take care of everything that needed to be done on the home front.

'I was never too involved in his work, or what he used to do', says Vimla.

'What he was earning, how much, where he was going, never bothered myself with these things. I was always more oriented towards taking care of the family – looking after our kids, our home, their health and my health – these were my only concerns. I think because of this, even he was able to concentrate more freely on his work, and never used to worry about household things.'

Praveen was born in 1975. When Praveen was a year old, Devendra was called to London, to join the Sussex University as a research scholar.

It was Vimla who was his inspiration in a way. Her father, brother were doctorates, Devendra knew these were things to be proud of. A research opportunity was his dream come true.

For Vimla, it was the pain of separation that mattered, for her… that her husband was in London did not mean anything too big. Her brothers too were in England and in her mind's eye, it was just a place where men went to study, work. The children recall a conversation, when Devendra returned home on a first visit from the UK. The conversation between the husband and wife went something like this:

Devendra: I got into an escalator.

Vimla: What's that?

Devendra: It's a moving stairs.

Vimla: Yeah, you found only me to make a fool out of. Moving stairs, huh.

So innocent was Vimla that when she went to live with Devendra in Sussex for a year, hilarious were some of her first encounters with foreigners.

Vimla recalls, 'We were in our room when there was a knock on the door.

'Devendra was in the washroom, and the children were studying. So, instead, I went ahead

and opened the door and there was a white person at the door, an *angrez*.

'I got scared out of my wits, what will he say to me? And then the man started talking and I got even more scared. But I made out that he was saying something like "tea" "tea leaves"…. But I was not sure, so I ran upstairs to where Tyagi was in the washroom.

'I told him there is an angrez at the door, don't know what he wants, maybe he said something like "tea."'

Devendra told me, 'Oho, what…? Ask him to sit down, or tell him you don't want anything. Tell him to get out and close the door.'

'No, no, I can't tell him to get out, no. What if he is someone!'

Irritated, Devendra said, okay and he wrapped himself in a bathrobe and came down to see who it was. Then the guy again started saying something in English. Devendra said something back in return, went into the kitchen and came out with some tea leaves in a bowl and gave it to him. They then exchanged a few more words and the man left.

'Devendra then closed the front door and told me I was right, he had come to ask us whether we had tea leaves. He wanted to make some tea. He was our neighbour.

'I was surprised, why was a white man asking us for tea? I wondered, here too they ask and borrow?'

Devendra would tell Vimla, 'Areeye fool, so

what if he is white? It doesn't make any difference. You should not be scared of the English. You must not think that they are above or you are beneath them. English to them is the same as Hindi is to us. Would you not be able to talk and write in Hindi fluently?'

'I said, yes, I would.'

'So, they are also like that. They are no more different from us than someone from South India is different from us. The guy is a neighbour and he is a professor in some college.'

'He had later asked Devendra who I was, whether I was his wife and he had said yes. He had told the professor, I did not know English and so was not comfortable talking to him. The guy had laughed, then he had said he could teach me English if we didn't mind. He lived just next door.'

This was followed by a funnier incident the next day. Devendra liked Dinesh, Vimla's brother, because of his free attitude and openmindedness. He was a liberal person and party around outside. Dinesh was married to a British woman, Anne, which was all very rare at the time. Dinesh would look after any family member who visited UK and was always very generous with his hospitality. He had looked after Devendra, when he first arrived in the UK. Devendra was attached to Dinesh, not only because of his charming personality but also because of his academic background. In some ways, Dinesh was Devendra's role model.

Dinesh was very strict, even when Vimla was a child. He would scold her for little things. People were scared of him because he was short tempered. But Devendra had a rapport with him like no one else did, they became very good friends. Dinesh often said, he would only come to India for Devendra. Dinesh had chosen Devendra as his sister's husband. There was something about Devendra that helped people relax around him, become comfortable and be his friends.

Dinesh and his wife Anne came to see Vimla and Devendra the next day. Vimla recalls, 'Both DS and DC were sitting together in the evening when Devendra mentioned what had happened the previous night. 'That the neighbour who was English had come to the door to ask for some tea, and I had got scared and had come running to him.'

Devendra liked to tease Vimla and he would not miss an opportunity to make fun of her. On this occasion, he said things which he knew would make her brother's blood boil. Devendra told Dinesh, 'the guy was saying that he would teach your sister English, he was calling her over to his house so that he could teach her English'.

Dinesh was very angry, and said out loud, and in Hindi (so that Anne Bhabhi doesn't understand what he was saying), 'Saale angrez, pehle meri India loot gaya ab meri behen ko lootega!' (The wretched English, first they looted my country, now they are eyeing my sister.) However, sensing

the mood, Anne looked very worried. Dinesh then looked at Vimla and said, 'now you will go to him to learn English?'

'Areeye, what am I supposed to do…? My husband is saying whatever nonsense is coming to his head. He is just poking fun at me, you relax.'

'I will break his (the neighbour's) bones!' Dinesh threatened.

'"Areeye! You are a doctor of bones and you are talking of breaking them!", Devendra told him. Dinesh had actually become very angry, "anyone dare talk about my sister!"'

Praveen talks of his flamboyant mama, and recalls how close his father had been to this doctor mama. 'I remember an incident when I had gone to pick up my mamaji with father from the station. He was supposed to come from Kanpur. I saw him at the train door, standing wearing a cowboy hat like the ones Clint Eastwood would wear, with a large overcoat, and then he came up to me and said, "Do you feel lucky, son", then give me a present or something. So he was that kind of a person, chilled out and flamboyant. He gelled well with educated people and those who had a thought beyond that which ties them to the age and generation they belong to. My dad was exactly that kind of a person.'

However, Vimla did not like it much in England. She would have to stay inside the house, with windows closed at all times. If she opened

the windows, cold winds would blow through. The owners of appartments would ask the Indian family to keep the widows closed, and this was culturally uncomfortable for Vimla. 'I liked open air better. I like staying in a place where there is a courtyard, where I can open windows, otherwise I feel suffocated. I would tell him I didn't like it much here in London', Vimla remembers.

Devendra would say, 'What! But people in India die… are desperate to come here'.

'Yeah, then you bring those who are desperate, why are you bringing me?'

Vimla did not like travelling to foreign countries much. So here they had their differences.

Their daughter Prerna recalls, 'Dad wanted her to come to Italy, Rome, he really wanted her to come. But she did not like going out like that. She would find some excuse or the other. She kept saying, NO. She was never into travelling. Even when I was older and in college, and she could leave us children, had she wanted to, she could have travelled with Dad. But she never wanted to. She liked staying back at home itself'.

Their younger son Praveen recalls, 'Our father used to travel quite a bit. Once or twice a year, but at that time it was considered to be a lot. I remember he went to Italy, Japan, Mexico, Brazil, US, UK, China, Sri Lanka, Bangladesh, South East Asian countries as well to places like Malaysia, Philippines etc.'

Despite disliking travel, Vimla had travelled with Devendra to quite a few places. They once went to China as part of an Indian delegation.

She had worn a saree and bindi on her forehead, making heads turn wherever she went in China. But Vimla disliked going with Devendra on his official tours.

'He took me to China, I could not understand the culture there. I could not stand strong smells. At these places, I had to be with him, around him… beer, alcohol, cigarettes, all these I could not bear, my head could not take these smells', is how Vimla puts it.

They went to Hong Kong and Singapore. Devendra sent Vimla tickets for Italy once, but 'at the time, Prerna had her exams and so, I did not want to leave her alone. He used to be sad that I would not accompany him to all the places he was travelling around the world. He would tell me, "I think you will come with me once she gets married. But he himself left us when she got married"'.

A colleague and family friend, VN Mishra says, 'From 1968, I was witness to Devendra's life. In 1969, we were in Vallabh Vidyanagar (Gujarat), when our book together came out'. Devendra was quite a scholar in his own right, with 40 papers and several books to his credit. Among these were: *Significance of the new strategy of agriculture development for small farmers,* Agroeconomic Research Centre, Sardar Patel University, Ballabh Vidyanagar, VS Tyagi,

DS Tyagi and VN Mishra,1969; *Managing India's Food Economy: Problems and Alternatives*, DS Tyagi, Sage Publications,1990; *Agriculture Price Policy*, AS Kehlon and DS Tyagi, Allied Publishers,1983; *Increasing access to food: The Asian Experience*, DS Tyagi & VS Vyas, Sage Publications, 1990.

Vimla's brother, RC Tyagi has this to say about Devendra's foreign sojourns, 'I would call him and ask him to get this and that from London for me; jackets, transistors and such things, not readily available in India at that time'.

Devendra would get it, 'but then, he would tell me you keep asking me to get these things from London. What is this? You do an MA in Economics, then do a PhD or MBA and go to London yourself and get these things on your own'.

'So, I did MA in Economics. But I could not do MBA from London because of the political situation there. Thatcher was in power, a conservative government, and they did not allow Indians to come to the UK as readily as before. My visa got cancelled even though I had secured an admission in MBA over there.'

'I told my jijaji (brother-in-law Devendra) this and asked him, what should I do now?'

'He then advised me to come into his line of profession. Do a PhD, he advised.'

'But I was sceptical, I did not know anything much. Even though my father, in his time, had done a PhD in Sanskrit, although his PhD was written in English. He was a great scholar.'

'On Devendra's advice, I took up a project at the Giri Institute of Developmental Studies in Lucknow. I started my career there and started a job there. While working there, I was in constant touch with my jija. He advised me then to focus my work on agro-based industries. So, I thought of doing a PhD on that and did it under a professor Mishra in Giri University. It was Devendra who had told me to do my PhD only under Prof Mishra, and had asked me to go meet him. I then started doing my PhD on India's sugar industry. And I would take a lot of help and advice from Devendra. I would write a chapter, and instead of showing it to my guru Professor Mishra, I would show it to my paramguru DS Tyagi because I had more faith in him. Chapter by chapter I compiled my PhD, showing them to jijaji time to time. When I had it completed, he crosschecked it. When I showed it to Professor Mishra, he asked whether I had shown it to anyone, and I said DS Tyagi. He said then, 'what is there for me to see in here if he has already seen. So, then I submitted my thesis', Vimla's brother says.

VIMLA AT THE DELHI DURBAR

ON THEIR RETURN from the UK, the Tyagi family began living in Delhi on a more permanent basis. They lived in a house in Munirka and Devendra took up a job with the government.

One day, in the morning, Devendra asked suddenly, 'where are the kids?'

'I told him, what do you mean, I've sent them off to school.'

Vimla recalls, how he had an astonished look on his face. 'What, to school?! At such a young age!', he said.

'Yeah, to school, what do you think… if I didn't study, my children too will not? You forget the family from which I come, it has always been about studies for them.' It was the city girl Vimla speaking.

Recalling his days on the family's return from the UK, Prashant, their elder son, says, 'I was born in Gujarat in 1970. We came back from England where we were for a year, and then came to live in Munirka. We were little kids then. Those were good memories'.

The first DDA flats were being built then, 'so it was nice, we liked it, our neighbours were good, and Delhi at the time was also safe. Not like how it is today. Then we moved to Kidwai Nagar, which was also a good government cottage, and Delhi also started growing, spreading its wings. Also, Delhi started becoming unsafe, unpleasant incidents kept occurring...happening here and there'.

Devendra made quick job moves at this time. From Lucknow to Gujarat, from there to the State Trading Corporation and to do a PhD, then to the Agricultural Pricing Commission. He soon became a rising government bureaucrat. The family's housing became better with Devendra's job advances.

Devendra's father suggested that he should take his nephews to live with them in Delhi. They had been allotted a bungalow, so the family back in the village wanted Devendra to take the kids with him and raise them up with Devendra's young family so that his brother's children would also get a good education. The eighties were aspirational times, people were beginning to move out of the villages, the quest for good education was urgent.

Vimla recalls that visit to the village. 'At the time Devendra had said yes... yes, nodded his head along, but when we were about to leave, he

immediately got into the rickshaw with me and took off.'

Vimla says, she tried calling for the children... Kamal and Deepak... 'but he shushed my voice and immediately left without them... Arey, call them too, they are also gonna come with us right?'

Devendra's quiet answer was, No!

Vimla asked him, 'But didn't your father ask us to bring the kids along with us too?'

'Oh you don't understand, you know that had we brought them with us... neither you nor I would have had a problem with it. But you have a habit of scolding our children. You pull Prashant up for misbehaving without a second thought. You will probably be the same way with your nephews too, because it's in your nature... to be strict and to scold. But that could later become a problem for us. They (the children's parents and grandparents) would come and say, is this why we sent our children to your place? To be scolded and beaten up?'

'Arey! You should have said this to them there! Why are you doing this now? Now your father will think something else.'

Vimla did not like Devendra not bringing the brother's children with them after saying yes. She gives this is an example of how diplomatic Devendra was as a person. He would say yes to something in order to not let people feel bad, or to not raise the issue at the time, but then later would do something else. Vimla did not understand this

behaviour. 'I would rather the person be upfront about what he thinks, says and does. If it's a yes… it's a yes.'

Daughter Prerna, recalling their growing up years, says, 'My dad would involve himself in our studies, especially mine and Prashant's. Praveen not so much. He would be strict with us, and give us a good scolding even if we got a few marks less. But Praveen would never get scolded. We would often protest this injustice, and cry foul'.

Vimla, of course, has a different story to tell. 'Even at home Devendra would not interfere much, he would not scold the children. He would always be too accepting of things.'

Vimla would just be too engrossed in her own self to pay attention to anyone else. She enjoyed walking so much. 'I never even took his government-allotted car to go pick up fruits and vegetables from the market. I would walk there myself and get those things myself. Others would be really surprised by this.'

'I think these small things make a good impression on your children, and they learn how to manage their own work. I would help in cleaning the house, even though by this time there were house helps to do those kinds of things. Prerna would see me and it would give a good impression, you know. I would even give the broom to Prerna and ask her to clean her own room. It's important to instil these qualities in your children', Vimla reminiscences.

'It was such a good time. I used to be called *memsahab*, he was always called by everyone as *sahab.'*

But Devendra never had any complaints, even when he was not happy or uncomfortable with someone or something. He had a lot of patience and would put up with anything with a broad smile plastered on his face at all times. He would try to get along with everyone and get everyone along with him as well, says Vimla, still puzzling over why such a man should be brutally shot on his daughter's wedding day.

Praveen recalls a tragedy that took place when they were in school and lived in Kidwai Nagar, 'Indu Mausi passed away. We remember that our dad had made a "trunk call" to Kanpur when this happened'.

Vimla's sister, Indu, was adamant after marriage to still sing and practice, and that led to domestic abuse, so much so that later she was driven mad.

Indu gave birth to five children, and still continued to hold on to her aspirations and dreams. Indu, consequently, suffered from depression as she was forced to let go of all her favourite hobbies, following marriage. Finally, she committed suicide. 'I was very sad when this happened. Possibly the same thing could have happened to me if I didn't get the kind of love and support I got in my marriage, which Indu did not. Indu also did not get any support from our natal family – under the

circumstances, what was our mother supposed to do or say? She did nothing and we all let Indu die by our silence', Vimla today says regretfully.

Vimla too could not pursue dancing because of her commitment to her young family, and that has always remained with her as a sad aspect of her life. She gives the example of Asha Bhosle after this. 'She was mistreated by her in-laws and her husband and was not allowed to pursue her musical dreams. She would be abused for practicing and doing *riyaaz* at home. She ultimately ran away with her two kids while she was pregnant with the third', Vimla points out, comparing her sister and herself with Ashaji.

'But I could never do such a thing, where would I run to? And after marriage, I could never get into dancing because of my children', Vimla adds, admitting, she herself was not as adamant about her dancing as her sister was about music and other such activities.

However, as a senior bureaucrat's wife, life began to subtly change for Vimla without her knowing the when, why and how of it.

Devendra came from a rural background, he was one with nature. He was always happier doing things that were related to farming and agriculture. He was tied to it from his roots, always loved farmers more. He wanted always to better the farmers' lot, if it was within his power to do so.

Devendra added cost to Agricultural Pricing.

Both Vimla and Devendra believed, 'it's important to also note at what cost we are purchasing from farmers, to ensure that they recovered their investments and have some money to feed their families'.

'Ours is a country of farmers, of agriculture. What about that? They are the only people who are not treated with respect', Vimla points out.

'I have not been able to study at all, and still I feel I can rule the world. I don't know from where that feeling comes. And I know it's not right to think that way, that I needed to have studied, that studies are important, and yet I feel that way', Vimla says.

'I would give certain suggestions to my husband, and ask him to put that forward in his meetings, or implement them. I don't know from where these thoughts come', she adds.

'I also have a habit of saying things upfront. What a person is, and what a person says, I am good at putting a mirror right in front of them', Vimla admits.

But Devendra was completely different, would not say anything to anybody to antagonise them. He would be good to everyone, not suspecting anyone. 'I don't think such an attitude is good. You should be at least a little imposing', says Vimla.

Vimla also recalls that in those days, though Devendra was a senior government official, he allowed his staff to bring their children to office.

There were no daycare or creches in offices, certainly not in government offices. Devendra would sometimes allow his staff to bring their children to work, and they would just play around and shout and do all sorts of things which children do.

'We are now getting so influenced by the West we are only borrowing what their culture teaches them. But we should not be doing that' Vimla says.

'We have become a country, a society which is only concerned with getting money and running off with it. Not concerned with the work we are doing.'

'If someone takes up a work, he should be completing it, doing it with his full vigour and energy. But no, their main concern is to just display a perceived sense of work, enough to get them their money and then run off with it.'

'Studies also don't teach this. Government is paying so much to its employees, and what are they doing? Sitting idly. Is this what their studies have taught them? Maybe, these were the things I used to tell him which Devendra liked. Because I was always inclined more towards practical work', Vimla recalls her time with Devendra.

'He was born in a village. He rose from there to become an educated man… just like that… he rose through the ranks to become the chairman of his organisation. His family was connected to agriculture. My family was connected to education. He combined both of them and became the best of both worlds.'

'My life with Tyagi was a completely family oriented one. The only thing outside of my family was when I would go for walks to Lodhi Garden. I would walk two and half hours there. I would do my household work myself, only very late in our life did we have household help to do the house work. I was not from a very rich household, was the daughter of a professor, so knew the value of money and also had important values instilled in me from my parents.'

'For others he was such a big person, Chairman and all that, but for me he was just my husband who would go make me tea when I was sad or unhappy. He would sometimes get down to wash clothes. He would start sweeping suddenly, if he would spot cobwebs somewhere or something like that.'

'We had a very happy and loving life together. He was not commanding like some other husbands are.'

'I never had any greed or want of money, and nor did he. If we had to go buy something from Khan Market, we would walk over there, rather than take the vehicle.

'I was never into taking care of money. I would not know where he kept his money, when he would go out on tours. He would give me money to keep, and I would forget about it. I would then call him and tell him I need money for this, and he would be like, you forgot again, it's there in the almirah under this or that item of clothing or the drawer.'

In traditional Indian households, the mother-in-law gives away her gold and jewelleries to every daughter-in-law in the house. 'So, I got my share in a bag. I did not know what to do with it, so asked him what I should do with this. I got this from your house', Vimla says.

'He said, keep it, it is a family heirloom kind of a thing. This is ancestral gold.'

Then Vimla goes on to say, 'but I was never attached to anything. I had even taken it to the jeweller to get it pawned, or remade it into another piece of jewellery for Prerna at the time of her marriage.'

Devendra was kind of taken aback at this, Vimla adds, remembering, he had said, 'what are you doing!'

VIMLA AND THE UNDERCURRENTS

ON THE SURFACE, the family was a picture of tranquillity. Vimla, the typical Indian housewife, taking care of the family; the man earning, career-oriented; children going to school; a family popular with friends and neighbours, living in the heart of the Indian capital.

When Vimla lived in Kidwai Nagar, the political climate in the country began to change. The late 1980s became one of the most turbulent periods in India's political history. Militancy began to plague the northeast, the northwest and the south of the country. Internally, left opposition too became militant. Vimla, innocent of all politics, continued to live happily, but it was not going to be forever after. Hers was not destined to be that kind of a story. No one knew that, nor did she ever imagine anything different.

'I once got a call from someone who said he was a doctor Pranav, calling from a hospital, saying that my husband has fallen down and has been seriously injured, that I should immediately come and see him.'

'First he said I've seen you go out for walks. You are her only. You are Vimla. I am a doctor. Your husband has met with an accident.'

'The entire time, I was asking the man... who are you... this must be a wrong number or something. But then, when he said... my husband had met with an accident, that's when I got concerned', recalls Vimla.

Vimla then called his office, asked his PA whether Devendra had reached office. He said, 'I don't know'.

Vimla then told the PA, 'what do you mean, find out, it's serious'.

So, the PA found out where Devendra was and called Vimla and told her, 'yes he is here. He is attending a meeting, a cabinet meeting'.

Vimla told him to get Devendra on the phone. 'I insisted. When he said Devendra could not come out of a cabinet meeting, I still insisted that he be called to the phone.' When Devendra finally called home, he sounded agitated, saying 'what is it?'

'I told him about the strange phone call I had received.'

'He said, stop worrying about these stupid things. There are a lot of such jobless people in Delhi who call and harass people without any cause or reason.'

'At that time Praveen was not well, he had an upset stomach and so needed constant tending to…which is why I first thought of calling his office and did not go directly to the hospital. If I had left… imagine what could have happened', Vimla shudders, recalling that day.

Soon other odd things like this began to happen. Vimla would get worried but Devendra paid no heed to all this.

'Once, I had gone for a walk in Lodhi Garden and was coming back when a Sikh person suddenly grabbed hold of my hand and started saying I was fortuitous, that my lines are really good, I will go to America. He held my hand and saw me from up close. I told him to leave my hand, what is this behaviour.'

'We should have understood what was going on, then', Vimla adds as an afterthought.

'We also used to have fights sometime because he would go out so often. I would tell him no need to take another project out of India. He would say to his friends, see my wife is jealous of my success.'

Vimla was tired of living alone and taking care of the children all on her own. 'I wanted him to be with me, how is that jealousy? I knew too much success was not good. I am also the daughter of a professor, and that too a big scholar. But my father didn't go out too much. Why did Devendra have to be this way?'

Their son Prashant recalls, 'Then we moved to

Bharti Nagar, which was again a good government house. But Delhi was becoming more and more unsafe. So we saw, over the years, Delhi growing but at the same time also deteriorating'.

'Then the 1983-84 Indira Gandhi-Sikh thing happened. We saw the situation then… how bad it was.'

'We knew at the time there would be repercussions for this, someone will have to pay for all the bad things that were happening, and people would be paying the price for it… we just didn't know that we would also be the ones paying a price for it eventually down the line.'

Praveen, their younger son, also recalls living for two years in Kidwai Nagar and then moving to Bharti Nagar, which was a very good locality for raising children. 'Nowadays, government servants do not get accommodation there easily…both the localities have become very posh.'

VIMLA AND THE DISTANT PEER GROUP

ONCE THE FAMILY moved to Bharti Nagar, Vimla used to go for walks to Lodhi Garden, and sometimes, Devendra used to accompany her on her walks, especially if it was a Sunday.

'I think, it was then that other officers and their wives started noticing me. But I used to be lost in my own thoughts and keep walking, or doing my exercises, not paying heed or attention to anyone.'

'That's how the other officers and their wives started recognising me as Tyagi's wife', Vimla says.

'Most people I knew, I met them at Lodhi Gardens. They saw my face every day and soon became friends. They would greet me everyday, but I was mostly lost in my own world.'

People used to call out, 'Oh, today also Tyagiji is not here'.

'Oh, has he left again.'

'Oh, he's not here in Delhi again.' Devendra would tell Vimla, they are all jealous.

'But I used to think why he has to take up so much work and be away from the family so much.... I would never know when or where he would apply to go to different places. He was a very strange person... I could never figure out what was in his mind as such.'

Some of the people I met would make remarks like, 'Madam, Tyagiji has again left the country, out for something'.

'I would find it odd. I would tell him this, ask why he went out so much?' Devendra would tell Vimla to shrug it off, 'these people are just jealous because I am getting so much work but they are not'. These things put doubts and suspicions in a wife's mind, Vimla admits. 'I would tell him so, but he would just say... knock it off.'

'We officers' wives living in that colony used to bring vegetables and food to each other's places and cook together. We, the wives, would interact like that, we would exchange food.'

'Vasudevan would appreciate my cooking', Vimla recalls.

'One day Vasudevan walked up to me and told me he liked my curry, *kadhi*. I didn't know them at all, Devendra never introduced me to them properly, he was weird that way.'

Devendra was a very strange kind of person, very simple too. 'If there was no vegetables in the house, I would tell him so, he would say, so what, just make *dal*. If I wanted curtains, he would say,

we need to keep moving forward in life. "Buying curtains means you are wanting to settle down in one place and I don't want to do that." So very simple. Just wanted to read books and work.' He did not care about any other material possessions.

All the officers' wives were more educated than Vimla, 'but they still respected me for who I was. I was even the chairman of their club, would preside over it. I had made a name for myself among all his friends', Vimla says proudly.

Devendra became friends with some of those people because of Vimla, and he would also take their help sometimes to solicit favours for his relatives. Once, Mrs Tripathi came to Vimla and said, 'did your *Jethani* send you a new saree or what?'

'What, why would she send me a saree?'

'Well bless your innocent heart, because of your husband's request your *jeth* (Satbir) has now been transferred to Kanpur. He is in a much better post now.' Devendra had asked Tripathi to do this and hadn't even told Vimla about it. She got to know about it from Mrs Tripathi.

Devendra would tell Vimla to come with him to this place and that, for outings, to meet his friends.

'I would say no, what will I do? You will order lemonade for me. I don't want any more lemonades. There will be other officers' wives too, you can talk with them.' The couple's conversations were classic.

'It is good I am not there. If I am at these get-togethers, I'll notice what the other wives are

wearing, saree and all, then you'll have to buy me one too.'

'Yeah, you see the saree, I will see the one wearing the saree. I can buy you a saree, but then you won't look like she was looking.'

'Like who was looking?' Vimla would reply angrily.

Devendra would then say, 'come, let's go and have some tea. Let's go for a walk to Khan Market'.

Vimla: You saw the *jhumk*a she was wearing?

Devendra: Jhumka, what jhumka?

'I was focused on the one wearing the jhumka. ...So, these kind of conversations would happen between the two, fighting mockingly, jokingly.'

'Now, with whom will I talk like this?' Vimla asks.

Vimla to Devendra: You go abroad every day. Other officers are not getting so much work, how are you getting so much work? Tell me the truth, where are you going?

Devendra: Oh those stupid officers, they don't know how to work... which is why they don't get the work. Only I can do it, I have to go.

Vimla: What do you do, math?

Devendra: Yeah, I can't do math here. You do it, count the number of kids.

'After marriage, your world becomes your husband. What he is doing, where is going, who he is going with. You can't do what you want to do on your own', says Vimla.

Devendra: Who was that woman you were talking to?

Vimla: She is Mrs Vasudevan.

Devendra: What!? How do you know his wife?

Vimla: What do you mean, we go to buy vegetables together.

Similar was it with Mrs Tripathi. 'So, Devendra also became friends with a lot of people because of me', Vimla reminiscences.

Today, Praveen too talks of the affectionate relationship his parents had.

'Father and mother's relationship was sort of a healthy one. Of course, there would be fights once in a while, but majorly they would be happy together. They would go for walks together in the evening. Would go shopping together. Go to temple together on Tuesday, my father went to mandir every Tuesday. They were happy together.'

'My dad would try to teach her new things, like learn English or drive a car. She would like that, appreciate that, but never actually did learn anything properly. She would be more interested in looking after the house and the family.'

'My mom never gelled with anyone from my father's side of the family. But my father had high regards for my mom's side of the family', Praveen recalls.

'My mother never liked going to the village much. We, as kids, were also not very excited or happy at the prospect of going to my dad's village.'

A village chief, Gram Pradhan, talks of

Devendra in great admiration. 'Devendra never acted like he was a chairman or anything.'

The people in the village were very proud of his achievements. Whenever he used to come back to the village, everyone would be happy to see him, and he would also talk with everyone in the humblest manner. Devendra would never act like he was a big shot government person. 'A simple man, he would sit with us on the floor, eat there, or discuss with us like we were old friends, with no hint of arrogance or anything.'

'When he was shot dead, people realised how important a post he had held. Because the news of his death was carried in most of the leading national newspapers, on TV, and that's when the people here realised what an important person he was in the Government of India. Before, we just knew he was in a high post... but never realised how important it was', the Gram Pradhan, an old school friend, says.

'It's hard to describe how the atmosphere became here in the village upon hearing the news of Devendra's death. Everyone assembled at his house here in Khilwai, there was no space to even stand in the courtyard, such was the turnout of the people. There was a pall of gloom for a long time in the village', the village official recounts regretfully.

Devendra's son Praveen recalls, 'But my dad loved going to the village. So, he would make sure that we would at least go there once in a year during vacations.' Devendra always made sure that

his children were also in touch with his family in the village.

'And, when we would come back from there, I would notice my mom and dad having an argument over something which must have happened at the village, something someone would have said which she would not have liked, and my dad would not have said anything to them.'

'But my father would rarely go to Kanpur. So, I remember only us children and mother spending time in Kanpur with our cousins there. My mom would be happy there, and we would also be happy because we had cousins of the same age there. So, *nani ghar* was fun.'

Recalling his days of growing up in Delhi, Praveen says:

'I remember, our house in Munirka didn't have anything... From there we shifted to Kidwai Nagar, and today it's very difficult for a government employee to get a flat there, they don't get housing there easily.'

'We stayed there for two years, and from there we went to Bharti Nagar, which was a very good place to raise kids and have a family. Good neighbours, locality everything. My mom made good friends over there, with the wives of other IAS and IPS officers, and through her friendships my dad got to know more people as well. So, she also helped him with advancing his network. Thus, my mom also played a part in introducing our family

to the good quarters of the society.'

Vimla reminiscences, 'He would meet with important people while we would go out for walks'.

Devendra would talk in English, would exchange friendly words. Vimla never concerned herself devendra's professional life and carrer, nor his earnings. Nor would Devendra come home and show off what a big personality he was, or how much he had earned or anything. Very simple.

'On the contrary, I would be the one acting all important', Vimla says.

'I would complain to him about the children, get angry. He would say, Oho... what has happened Madam Home Minister, what has happened? What's troubling you?'

'See, the children, how much they are troubling me.'

Devendra would then call Prerna, ask her, 'what has happened, why are you doing this. Don't trouble your mother'. Then he would go into the kitchen and make tea for Vimla.

'I would be angry and he would try and make my anger disappear. He would always try to make others happy around him...'

Then who was this person who wanted him dead, how did he make such an enemy? Vimla asks. Destiny has to still answer that question.

Devendra would sing that song for Vimla, Waheeda Rehman and Raj Kapoor's *'Barfi ka sab ras le liyai re pinjrewaali muniya.'* He would call

Vimla Munni.

'I would say... what do you mean, my husband is a cage, a pinjra?'

'What else, you are in a cage only.'

'He would jokingly call me *'brahmachari ji ki naunvi santaan* (the bachelor's ninth child).'

'So he would talk to me about these things. Never about work-related things.'

'And with him I also became very satisfied and happy', says Vimla.

Praveen recalls those sweet-sour days of growing up and the atmosphere at home and interactions with their father.

As far as staying at home was concerned, 'Our father used to leave home at around 8:30 in the morning in his ambassador car, and would come back by around 7-7:30, sometimes later'.

Praveen says, 'and when he would come back home, he would still be working on office material, or reading economics magazines, or he would have guests over. So, those were the times when people from the neighbourhood also came visiting our house... they would sit and chat and discuss things'.

Those were the times when you didn't have cell phones, and rarely had TVs, so people indulged each other more. 'My dad loved having friends over to the house. So, a lot of socialising would happen, and he was a big-time social person. There were times when we had foreign visitors too. In that sense, the time shared with our father was less,

but it was still good and we were grown enough to understand the critical lessons of life.'

'He had a way of putting the right seeds in mind, even if he was spending only half an hour with us. It would make sense logically… whatever he used to say. So, I didn't need him to go out with me, play badminton with me, teach me cycling or skating, but he would teach me other important lessons in life. I would and could talk to him… like tell him, "you know dad, my hairstyle is bad, and people will make fun of me for it". He would start giving lessons through stories, parables.'

Devendra would tell his young son, 'People will make fun of you whatever you do, good or bad, they will find something wrong in every situation. So, you need to stop paying heed to what they are saying and focus on the important things. Our father had anecdotal ways of telling us what is wrong and what is right in life'.

Praveen admits, 'I was never a good student and my marks in school were always poor and very very low. I was more of a happy-go-lucky kind of person, not concerned with studies but just having fun, teasing my sister etc.'

'Our father was the most concerned about my sister's studies. He wanted more than anything else for my sister to become a doctor. Prerna used to speak very fluent Gujarati, and she would take part in debates and all that.'

'But my sister did not want to become a doctor,

and she turned out to be a genetics researcher' Praveen says, emphasising that Devendra's focus was mostly on the studies of his daughter and then towards his older son, 'me… not so much'.

'I was considered to be the little one in the house, and it would not matter whether I study or not because he could set me up somewhere or keep me with him wherever we go. So, if I got less marks, my father would say at least he didn't get zero, he got something so it's alright. But when my brother used to get like 99, father would get serious and scold him... why he lost that one mark!' Devendra seemed to have reconciled to the fact that one of his three children would not be a great performer.

'So, my elder two siblings were very studious and ahead of the curve. My sister was also very good at extra-curricular activities, debating, dancing etc. She was outgoing, my father would try and get her on the study table at all times, but she would do other things too. My brother kept to the study table always, wanting to get into IIT. It was also because of the group we were in, the colony we were living in. Bharti Nagar had all intelligent, smart, brilliant kids. Peer group matters too. So that probably affected my brother, motivated him to study', Praveen explains.

Devendra, an Officer Par Excellence

Praveen remembers his father's professional colleagues, like Bhalla and Goyal. 'Goyal was running an organisation called ISID (Institute for Studies in Industrial Development). He was the Chairman of ISID. It was a govt institute and it was set up so that researchers could do statistical research on industrial development. At the time, new computers were coming up, so this institute had a lot of them. I remember my dad would take me along to the place, and I would play games on those computers where others would do coding and other statistical research.'

Devendra's brother-in-law, RC Tyagi, recounts his time with Devendra in these words:

'When I was in the process of doing my PhD, I used to go to APC to meet him, to show him my chapters and seek his advice and all. There was a Professor Bhalla there in APC, and he used to come to our institute, Giri Institute from Delhi as a guest lecturer. So, when I would come to meet my jija, and see him, I would be impressed by the kind of people my jija knew. So, because I was in this line, I knew what kind of a position my jija was in; he was at the top.'

It was Devendra who had changed the name from APC to Commission for Agricultural Costs and Prices (CACP). Vimla's brother Umesh describes Devendra as a 'man of intellect', this is what Devendra's office colleagues said, adding that the position of chairperson of the Agriculture

Pricing Commission that his brother-in-law held was not awarded to even IAS-rank officers.

'When my PhD was in final stage, I went to his house once. He was taking a stroll in Lodhi Garden. It was almost the time of Prerna's marriage. One month before his assassination. I was walking back with him. I saw the different houses next to his with a lot of security.'

'I asked him who they belonged to. He said Police Commissioner and others. I also told him to get a security, he was living in such a VIP area after all. He said, "why should I take security?"'

'I answered back, "so that when I come to your place with my friends to meet you or my sister, they will get impressed seeing such a high security arrangement at the house. That my jija was such a big personality." But he replied to this, "but did you complete all your chapters?". After all, he was an academician at heart.'

'I said yes, I have completed, but I will show it to you tomorrow, I have just come to see you today…I have just come from Lucknow.'

'Devendra: Yes, your focus is not on studies but these trivial things only. Then he said, I am a master, a teacher, what do I need security for? These people are police officers, they deal with thugs and what not, and so they need security. Why do I?'

'So, he was such a simple person… that he did not consider himself as a very important person who could be threatened or harmed for any reason.'

'Next day he called me to his office chamber with my chapter. So, I took my thesis and went to his office. This was the first time I was visiting his office after he had become the Chairman, CACP. Outside, when the guard stopped me, I told him I want to meet the Chairman. When he placed the call to his PA, he said to send me in.'

'When I went there, I saw a very huge nameplate in brass with the name Dr DS Tyagi, Chairman. I knocked and entered. It was a huge office. I was very impressed. But I was a little surprised to see that there was a blackboard there. It kind of looked out of place to me. The office was so well decorated, there were so many phones on his table. Why was there a blackboard which looked strange to me.

'There were so many chairs opposite to his. But I said, I will sit on this one, which was beside his chair. He used to treat me like a younger brother, like I was still a child, and said yes yes, come here, sit beside me. I asked him about the blackboard, to remove it. He said no, it's important. I write things here, when there are meetings, I explain things here.'

'He would treat me like a child, I would ask him to take me seriously. I have written the final chapter of my PhD, please take a look.'

'Your mind is never towards studies but these stupid things. How come you wrote a PhD? Oh, now I understand... probably your wife must have written it for you'...that was Devendra, my jijaji.'

'Yeah, Kamlesh wrote it for me.'

'Well, then leave your PhD here, I will see it later.'

'What do you mean leave it here, so should I go then?'

'No you can stay if you want to, but what will you do? You will start to get bored once people start coming in. I usually stay very busy, there are so many people who keep coming to meet me. And that's what started happening, people kept coming in to meet him. So then I left for home. I told him, "don't lose my thesis." He said, "where will it go?", you go.'

'When he returned home that evening, he had my thesis with him. I asked about it. He said, "sit first, let's have tea" and asked Vimla to make tea.

'I then said I won't have tea with you, today I had tea with a very big and hot-shot personality. He was taken aback, and asked who I went to meet after I had left his office. Even then the thought did not occur to him that he was the big shot because he was such a simple person. I said I had tea with the Chairman of CACP, I am not having tea with you now. There I was served tea in bone china teacups, here you will give me in steel glass… I used to be so impressed by where he was, what he was. I felt very lucky that I was so close to him, that the Chairman of CACP was checking my PhD.'

VN Mishra was another person who would sit with Devendra Tyagi and discuss everything with him. 'I was in Papua New Guinea when he

became Chairman. But we were like brothers, and even when we were in different countries we would talk over the phone. He called me up and said he became Chairman', Mishra recalls.

'He also gave me advice on monetary terms. I once got a consultancy opportunity, which I did not want to take because it was not grade P5 (a government service grading). So, I went to Tyagi and told him this, that I did not want to take this assignment which had come from ADB (Asian Development Bank) because they weren't giving P5, I was going to decline the offer.'

'It was evening then, when I told him this. He agreed with me at the time and told me yes, decline this, they are not giving P5 so no need to take this offer. But he said send the declining letter tomorrow, what's the hurry? Then he distracted me from the subject and said, "let's go have some tea and samosa."'

Next day morning, first thing Devendra did was get into Mishra's office, direct. He then said, 'yesterday, I told you so because otherwise you wouldn't have slept well, would have kept worrying about this. But are you stupid? They are paying you well. What's this obsession with P5? Why do you need P5?'

'Stupid Panditji! Now send them your acceptance letter, I will be here to take care of things, you go for a year and earn money, go.'

Just the day before, he had agreed with Mishra wholeheartedly because he had not wanted to keep

the man awake and worrying. It was almost the end of the day when this conversation took place. 'Devendra was very practical also, and also very humorous.'

'I am yet to come across a person who had something critical to say about DS Tyagi', recalls Mishra. 'People, in fact, had problems with me, they used to say I scold other people and all that. But Tyagi was well behaved with everyone, juniors, seniors, and everyone loved him unequivocally. He had very clear vision and clear perception.'

Devendra Tyagi had also written several articles for the *Economic and Political Weekly* (EPW).

'We never had any political relations with anyone. We were basically government servants, serving the government to the best of our ability. There was no bias... at the time there was no RSS or anything, so no factions existed. We grew up thinking in a socialistic way. Tyagi was a free-minded person. He also came from a fairly affluent family, his family had a lot of land in their village, they had good produce', Mishra says in tribute.

'Whatever I used to show him he would see and give his insights...very sharp, technical mind...he also would give me his writings and thoughts for my opinion.'

'He always used to be very supportive and cooperative...we used to discuss about ways to earn money as well....used to do consultancies for it... Tyagi always used to say not to worry, focus on

work, do it properly, money will come.'

'When I got the ADB consultancy, Rao Birender Singh was the Chairman. He was a tough Chairman who would not give approvals for such projects easily, but because of Devendra Tyagi I was able to go. He assured the Chairman that he would take care of the work in India.'

'Since we were working for the government, we had to take permissions before publishing a paper. Once, at the time of Dharam Narain as the Chairman, I wanted to publish a paper. I sent an application to him for approval, around 20 days passed and I still had not received the approval for him.

'I told Tyagi, *yaar, abhi tak approval aaya nahi.*

'Oh don't worry, Dharamji *to aise hi hai, aaram se kaam karte hai apna*'.

'Then one day, we were both called into the Chairman's office. We went in and sat on the chairs, and were offered tea. Then Narain said to Tyagi, "I don't know what all you write and submit to me. You expect that you can submit anything and the Chairman sahib will correct your English? In that case, why don't you become the Chairman and see? And I will get to Mishra's paper. See, not every time will you get a good boss over you who is going to pass your papers. So, you need to be careful and all.'

The thing with submitting papers for approval is that one did not usually get approvals, because of professional jealousy or many other reasons.

Plus, the bosses and the government did not want anything policy-related to be published in the public domain. 'So, Narain advised us not to wait for approvals from anyone, but rather at the beginning of the paper to just add that "the views expressed in this paper are personal;."'

So, he was basically tipping us off. 'But as soon as we got out of the office, Tyagi laughed it off and said, *Arey lagta hai Buddha sathiya gaya hai. Tum tension mat lo.* (The old man has gone bonkers, you do not get tense.) That was what Devendra was like, never getting offended at anything, always taking things in a very light and funny way.'

'When he became Chairman, he called me and we recalled the day....Devendra said, Dharamji was correct in saying that someday we will also become Chairman, and see it has come true!'

'I was in Papua New Guinea at the time, and he called me back from there.'

After becoming Chairman, 'Devendra went to Mongolia, and this time I was here to take care of work while he went abroad', says Mishra.

'We sometimes used to sit and discuss about what is to be done next. What should I do after this, now that I am Chairman?, Devendra would wonder.'

'You see, while working for the government your academic life gets very restricted, and we were both academically inclined.'

'We used to think that let time pass now, and later

we will indulge in research and write more papers. Used to think, *kab tak zindagi bhar sarkar me rahenge?*

Devendra was very sharp and very intelligent, he was, in fact, known for that. Everyone used to go to him for advice, and he would willingly help everyone out. 'I once wrote a paper which I gave him for review. He read it and came to me, to my room, and gave his insight.'

'He said… rest everything is fine… but if I were in your place I would have started the paper by explaining about structure first, and then introduce levels later. You have directly started from level, where is the structure?'

'I could not understand, and asked him to explain. He said, c'mon panditji, how can you not understand structure, use your brain. You must use your brain, otherwise how did you write the paper if you can't understand this? Then he explained what he meant by structure. Then I got what he was talking about. So, he had this very sharp and analytical brain. Helped me with many things, used to tell me to clear my perception.'

'He used to order *rasgullas* at the office for us from time to time.'

'Once I was supposed to prepare a comment draft on a policy which was supposed to go to the PMO.

'I had written one page and thought I'll write another, prepare a two-page draft. Had very little time. Tyagi saw me struggling and asked what I was doing. Then said, *aarey*… are you mad or what…

tell me what does the PM want, what does he want to see?'

'I told him the subject, and that this is what he wants.'

'He said, see, I keep trying to make you understand and you still don't, you'll die like this only, if you don't understand Panditji. You will want your paper to be content driven and having several anecdotes and other such things, but these don't work in the government.'

'He said you are mad, give this to me, this is supposed to go to the PM, mad man, I will cut everything. You need to condense it all. You understand that even your secretary does not want to read more than one page of what you have written, do you think anyone in the PMO will read your verbose two-page draft? I don't want PhD thesis. Give him brief, to the point, and finish it.'

'Finally, when the paper went to PMO... they said we wanted exactly this, nice work!'

Apart from being so intellectually sharp and witty, Devendra was also a very good human being. 'When I used to get upset about anything, he would console me...used to say do you think every person you meet in your life will be good to you? So don't think about them.'

'Devendra was younger to me in age' Mishra says, 'but for me Tyagi was always like an elder brother, in many aspects', he adds.

THE BLOODBATH AND AFTER

WHY WAS SUCH a man shot dead on the day of his daughter's wedding? Who could have planned such a cruel fate for a diligent officer? For what reason? Devendra's family and friends still continue to puzzle over the who and why of it. After so many decades, the who does not matter so much but the why still hurts.

Recalls Prerna of her wedding day, 'I was studying in South Campus. My Principal at the time had her residence in the campus itself. So, she invited us for lunch. We were just five students, all girls in the batch. My father came to drop me to college that day, along with the driver, in the white ambassador car.'

'He asked me how long it would take. I told him an hour. But then we went for lunch, it took more than an hour, almost three hours because we were chatting, having fun and all that. And when I got out from the campus, I saw him standing at the same spot, where he had dropped me.'

'I felt so bad that I had made him wait.'

'But he did not say a word to me. I told him he should have left and all that, but he said it's alright, did not make me feel bad at all. It was, I think, on 8th May, just two days before the wedding.'

Prerna remember that day too vivdly. 'It was early in the morning, we had all woken up. I remember my dad coming into my room and giving me a tight hug. I was his *gudiya*. Maybe he was emotional at the time... that I was going to go away. Because this was not an everyday thing obviously, he would never randomly come and give me a hug, but that day he did.'

'I, for some reason, was in my parents' room, when suddenly I heard the gun shot. At the time I thought it must have been my baba (grandpa, Devendra Tyagi's policeman father), who had a habit of firing a gun in the air in celebration. I honestly thought baba must have come early from his hotel and fired the gun in the air. But then I heard the ruckus and everything....'

'I remember when I came back from the hospital, Prem *maasi* was sitting in the room with mother. There was an adjoining washroom in my mother's room, but I saw her walk out of the room and go to this other washroom at the far end of the house. I got scared, I had already lost my father, and I was scared if mother was also going to hurt herself, for she had locked herself in the washroom.

I started banging on the door asking her to open the washroom, and from inside I heard the breaking of glass and her crying.'

'One thing that she did that I remember was that everyone was telling her it's gonna be okay and all that. In my mind the two clear memories that I have was... one the gunshot that I heard, I thought it was Babaji firing a gun in the air. The other when mom… I saw her getting up, going to the back washroom, locking herself in the washroom… I remember my *mamaji* was sitting next to me, and then I got up and left after her, to see where she was going and what she was doing.'

'People were obviously coming and consoling me, but those are more of a vague memory.'

'I didn't even want to get married.'

'But my mom was convinced that that is what father would have wanted.'

'Also, in India, it is a big deal for a girl to get married, otherwise they think what will happen to her, what will become of her, what will she do in life, and once she is married then the worry is over. So that was probably what my mom must have been thinking at the time.'

'But neither me, nor Gaurav wanted to get married at that point… I was so devastated by the shock of the incident, we could have waited. But my mom was adamant. I remember her saying, …and she kept saying… "take her away, take her away". I remember her telling this to my *maasi*s…

that the marriage should not stop and it should go on like it was supposed to. And I didn't want her to be more worried than she already was.'

'If I didn't get married she would keep worrying over it. My mom probably wanted some sort of normalcy and to go ahead with things the way they were supposed to happen.'

'And life does not stop for you either.'

'There was no joy or happiness in anyone's face on that day. It was sort of like a duty, a ceremonial thing that we were doing just for the sake of it. Just a token that yes, we are married now.'

'Everyone from our family was there.'

'My cousin had flown in from London. He was originally not supposed to come for my wedding, but when he heard about my 'papaji' he took the first flight out of London. He couldn't get a direct flight to Delhi which was through Bombay. He had to take a domestic flight from Bombay to Delhi. So generally, anyone flying internationally and then taking a domestic flight goes through a security check and all that, but because he was my dad's relative and he had come for his funeral, he was allowed through immediately. He said he could hear through the speakers and callcomms, that Dr AC Tyagi is arriving from London and to give him immediate security clearance, and that's when he realised for the first time what an important person DS Tyagi must have been.'

'My *chacha* and *Tauji* were there, Virendar

chacha was there, some of his close friends were also there...but none of our extended friends from Delhi were there at the wedding. Then, of course, some of Gaurav's family members were there. He has two sisters, they were there. His parents.'

'We had the *saath pheres* and all that, *var mala*, all basic rituals carried out, but it was a very solemn affair. All the rituals that had to be done to make us husband and wife was done, but none of the celebratory parts of it was done. Like stealing the groom's shoes and all that.'

Vimla now recalls, 'before Prerna's marriage, we would get phone calls at home asking for her, someone saying he was some friend of hers. And she would never come to attend those calls, always saying she had no such friend who would call like this, it was not her friend'.

'I would talk to the guy, saying she doesn't want to come to the phone, and that she is saying you are not a friend. I would tell Prerna to at least see who it is, maybe it was her friend from college or somewhere else.'

'We even got a call from the guy at night, and Bhaisaab picked up the call and said, "what?" He then put down the phone. But he never paid no attention nor heeded such phone calls.'

'Maybe it was a sign, an omen or something', Vimla now says.

'I don't know what these things are indicative of, such calls, such omens. He should have been more careful, why was he always so dismissive

about such things? Maybe, this is why he got killed in the end.'

'BBC too had carried a news item on Devendra's death which was broadcasted in London. We got a call from my Anne bhabhi, DC Tyagi's wife who was in London asking about what happened. Devendra was a man of international stature', Vimla remembers.

'Devendra's brothers and sister soon began crying foul, saying the killer had come for Dinesh Tyagi… my brother... and instead got my husband.'

The incident created suspicion among the relatives as no one actually could guess why Devendra was killed.

"I heard the shot and not sure of what it was went to see. The first words that came to me was Bhaisaab, Bhaisaab! I could not say anything else. At first, I thought he must have just fallen down, because his blood pressure would sometime be low, maybe because of that... I thought', Vimla recalls the black moments.

'They shot him in the head, targeted his mind. There was so much money, cash, jewellery and other things in the house for it was our daughter's wedding. But everything was dust compared to his mind, that's the real wealth they went for', Vimla says.

'They killed him at a time when our house was full of gold and silver.' Only the lowest of people go after money and wealth, those who are smart and intelligent go for the real wealth, which is knowledge and power, Vimla adds.

Bharti Nagar was full of people after the incident. One could not even enter the colony in a rickshaw, it was so crowded. Praveen's school friends and teachers had also come.

Premonition

'According to the Pandits, the *muhurat* or the auspicious date for Prerna had not been on the 10th. Devendra convinced the pandit to take out the Muhurat on 10th. But the day was not a good day according to the astronomical charts. How Devendra got the 10th of May approved, I don't know', says Vimla.

Around 15-20 days before the marriage, after the marriage had been arranged, Vimla says, 'I started getting the feeling that we were being watched.'

'Someone would peek at us from behind the bushes. I would see someone standing outside our kitchen window. Or someone who I did not recognise standing near the laundry guy. I think I was being researched, and my children were being researched. What we do, where we go, what all our activities are.'

'Around a week before the wedding, our phone went dead. I would receive calls, but I could not make calls.'

'Prerna would get calls from guys, saying they are her friends. They would say, "Aunty ask her to at least talk to me." I would say she doesn't want

to, that you come home instead and maybe then she would recognise you. We would even get the call at 2:30 am at night. Devendra would scold us. Two days before the wedding, our phone lines went dead, we could only receive calls. Why did he never get suspicious?', a distraut Vimla now asks.

Sheetal Prasad was a member of Devendra's office staff who was present on the fateful day on the premises. He now claims someone has seen Tyagi Sahib's spirit roaming the offices of CACP.

Recounting the sequence of events Sheetal Prasad says: 'I was sitting in the lawn, having tea, when two sardars came on a scooter. One of them was tall and the other was short. Pant and shirt. They came and they immediately rang the bell.'

'I was having tea, and with me Fakir was also there. Then Tyagi sahib opened the door.'

'They asked him whether he was Tyagi. He said yes I am. They then asked him to step outside. Tyagi got a little irritated, but then he stepped outside. One man then took out the revolver and fired at him. The first shot hit him on his head and he fell down. I shouted what is happening. Fakir shouted that someone has killed Tyagi sahib. He ran after them outside. I ran inside to tell everyone.'

'Just before that, some guests had come from Kanpur, and they were inside. When I went inside, Mrs Tyagi was talking to them, saying see someone is bursting crackers for your welcome. I said no Madam, someone has shot Tyagi sahib. She got scared.'

'What are you saying?'

'I said yes Madam, come with me and see. And then we went and saw him lying on the floor.'

'Kohra sa mach gaya'.

'I tried looking at the shooters, to try and see the scooter number. But then they pointed the gun at me and I ducked and lay flat on the ground.'

'I later told the police everything that I saw. The police has also harassed me a lot to find out the truth. Taking me for the post mortem, then there had been a shootout in Paschim Vihar, and then they took me to identify the terrorists caught / killed there… whether they were the same.'

'But I never recognised anyone. Police said they killed one of them in an encounter.'

Sheetal says, police then forced him to identify the killers, telling him to identify a specific person, although he could not exactly remember Tyagi's killer's face.

'The taller sardar was the one driving the scooter. The shorter one shot him. But I didn't notice their faces properly. But then… the police said no, this is the same sardar. And so, I also had to be a witness and give my statement in the court saying that yes, this is the same sardar, even though I actually couldn't say for sure. They had caught a tall sardar and brought him to court and said this is one of the two. And I had to say yes.'

'Everyone else was inside. Fakir and I…we were the only two outside.'

'The previous night was very good. A lot of officers were there. It was a wonderful party.'

Recalling that Praveen had scolded the police, saying, 'what are you doing, what duty are you doing, terrorists came and killed my father', Sheetal Prasad points out, 'Bharti Nagar is a walled campus. When you go from Khan Market to Sai Baba temple, on the left side is Bharti Nagar and on the right, there are lanes in Lodhi estate, and on one of those lanes the police commissioner stays. So, basically, someone has to get out of the Bharti Nagar campus through a gate, cross the road, and then reach the police commissioner's house which is in one of the lanes there.'

'In the morning, Devendra was in a very jovial mood', Sheetal continues.

'I had stayed there the previous night along with Fakir Chand.'

'After Devendraji's death there were many who came from CACP to pay their respects. Vimlaji would tell us to keep an eye on these people, that she doubted all of them… PP Singhji was crying, and she would say, why is he crying so much? She suspected everyone. She would even doubt us…'

'Her mental state was disturbed. She once came to the office when Acharya sahib was Chairman. She saw him and said why are you sitting here, this is my husband's seat.'

'Because… officially it was a terrorist activity… the family got compensation from the government.'

But nothing can compensate for life, he adds.

Vimla's youngest brother RC Tyagi was also present at the scene of crime. 'I was very lucky to have known him', Rakesh says.

Rakesh was doing PhD under Devendra and so he was very sad as he was very close to his jijaji. Looked to him for advice.

'But luck runs out. I was supposed to come from Kanpur but had gotten late in arriving due to some work. I reached that morning. I had just reached his house and had gone inside.'

Devendra chided me, 'Oh, so you have come now, after everything. Missed yesterday's function.'

'I then went inside to wash my face and get fresh. My wife had already come, she was staying at a hotel. I was also supposed to go there and meet her there but had come here first. My jija said, "you have come now, I won't talk to you, don't talk to me." They were having tea.'

'I said, jijaji, I will win you back don't worry. I know you are upset and angry, but I will win you over. But where is my wife?'

'You go find her, I don't know.'

'The morning's conversation went like this. Those were my last words to him. I was offered tea, it didn't have sugar. I asked for sugar, "I'll get fresh and come", I said. So, I hadn't even drunk tea. I was washing my face inside when I heard the gunshots.'

'I thought... maybe kids were bursting crackers. I have come to a wedding house, maybe it was children bursting crackers. Then I thought... maybe my wife and kids had also come. I came to the hall and saw everyone running here and there. I went with everyone to the spot, saw Devendraji lying flat just outside the doorway. I was shocked.'

Rakesh continues with his sombre tale: 'I, Prashant and one of his friends got into his ambassador and took him with us to the hospital.'

'We didn't wait for the ambulance.'

'Devendra was with me on the back seat, was lying on my lap. We reached AIIMS. There, they started asking us what happened and everything. We then called our relatives. We knew a lot of doctors who were friends, started calling them. Dr GB Pant, Dr Sanjay... a crowd started gathering.'

'They gave us list of medicines to bring, this and that. We would bring everything. But everything which the doctors tried...it did not work. Some half hour later, the doctors came and said nothing can be done. They declared him brought dead.'

Rakesh recalls, 'Four shots were fired. Three hit him, one hit the door'.

'Police investigations began from all sorts of angle. They were looking at all the possible angles so as to not miss out on anything. But the final conclusion was that it was Khalistani terrorists.'

'Devendra's death was a loss to so many people... family as well as the people of India.'

'I feel it was a great personal loss for me, my sister feels it was a great personal loss for her. Similarly, everyone feels his life was a great personal loss to each one of them because he was such an important figure in everyone's life.'

'I felt my career would come to a standstill because of his death.... In our family, there has been no one at such a high position ever.'

'When I told him to get security, it was more out of a style requirement... to just show off. I didn't know how much weight and importance my words carried at the time...I myself did not imagine any threat to Devendraji from any quarter whatsoever. He was such a well-liked man.'

DS Tyagi always talked about studies, academics and gaining knowledge. He did not like talking about worldly, materialistic things. 'And listening to me talk about all the things that mattered to me, he would always tell me to instead focus on studies. So, when I told him to get security because it would look cool, he didn't know, nor did I, that this wasn't useless trivial talk, but was actually a very important suggestion I was making.'

He was succeeded by Acharya as the Chairman, and the government provided him with top security.

'I had done my PhD under my jijaji's guidance but he couldn't live to see me get my PhD approved. Yet, he used to call me Dr RC Tyagi. On the wedding card which I received for Prerna's wedding, he had written with his own hand, in

his handwriting, Dr RC Tyagi. My viva was after his death. Got my PhD after his death. I would think that if he has called me a doctor, then it means my PhD is completed. For me, his word was everything. That is what mattered to me more.'

'You don't anticipate something like this happening, so it was a shock for all of us', says Prashant.

'My friend who lived across our house brought his car out and we rushed him to AIIMS, but it was too late by the time we reached. I was in the car with RC Tyagi, along with my friend, Sanjay. Sanjay and I went to the same school.'

'Once we reached the hospital... within half an hour everybody else reached the hospital as well. But we were told soon that he was dead.'

According to Praveen, UC Tyagi, one of Vimla's brothers, was a criminal procedures doctor, a medical examiner. He had become a Chief ME in a government hospital. 'He was the one who had declared DS Tyagi dead. He had examined him.'

Was UC Tyagi in Bharti Nagar at the time of the shooting?

'No he wasn't there, he had just arrived in Delhi by a morning train', Praveen recalls. 'He got to know about the shooting from the cab driver who was taking him to Bharti Nagar from the station. Dinesh Tyagi, the eldest brother was there for one week.'

After Devendra was declared dead, 'We then

went back home, trying to deal with the event. People were all shocked, coming in, paying their respect and extending their condolences etc', Praveen says.

'In the evening there were still people who went to Hotel Samrat because they didn't know of the shooting, and then they came to our house with shock and disbelief showing on their faces. Nobody could grasp the reality of the incident, hardly able to make sense of it.'

'We lived in a well-protected, gated colony with other senior police officials having their residents there too.'

'This was the first incident that happened in Delhi like this. So, after this incident it became a huge issue, it was also raised in the Parliament and the police started taking stricter actions against the Punjab militants', says Prashant.

'In a way, our father's death acted as a catalyst for the cleaning up of the militancy in Punjab. But we had to pay the price for the political situation there.'

'The wedding ceremony in Ghaziabad was not really a festive occasion. We did it as best as we could do, under the circumstances. But we were glad that at least some things were going on according to what had been planned.'

'I graduated in May 1993. I had just got into my 4th year when the incident happened.'

'LK Advani came to our house after the incident, and we have picture of him in the front page of a

newspaper. He helped us too. He also wrote to the government, saying we should be allowed to stay in our government flat.'

'After the incident happened, immediately, Babbar Khalsa claimed that it was their doing and the reason they stated was that they wanted to go after all the ministries and those involved who were against the Punjab farmers.'

'Manchanda, who was the chief engineer of Doordarshan, was similarly killed. So they were going after soft targets. They claimed this, but the police denied it.'

'When such high profile killings take place and terrorists involvement is said to be there, the police also comes under a lot of scrutiny.'

'So they inevitably try to suggest that there is a family feud. In my father's case, they went all the way, investigated me, my sister, our brother-in-law, looked into family feuds, any land disputes, any loans my dad had, but after everything… they said they couldn't find anything.'

'And after that they said the investigation is still going on.'

'The one thing that happened was that the people who allegedly did the shooting were killed within two weeks of the incident. They had run to somewhere in Rajasthan and they were tracked down and then firing took place and they were killed or taken by the police and there was an encounter somewhere in the desert.... These were

theories that the police then forwarded. At the same time, they claimed, "the incident was still under investigation."'

Praveen, the youngest among the three children says, 'My father was always busy making sure people were happy and setting them up in fine hotel rooms, looking after their comfort. Other than that, he was very fond of his sisters, would go and chat with them a lot. Would burst into laughter with his family. He was happy to be a common man.'

'On 9th and 10th May, everyone was happy. People were staying in Hotel Samrat. We had initially booked in Hotel Ashoka, but the booking got cancelled because of some error, and then my dad booked in Samrat instead which was right next to Ashoka. So there were people staying there. So going back and forth to there and the house. There was a pandal. So celebratory things kept happening all day on the ninth.'

'On the wedding morning we woke up… people were sharing jokes. There was a dholak also, some ladies were singing songs. Prerna was inside. All this was happening when we suddenly hear the shots.'

'I ran outside to see what it was, and saw my father lying on the ground, with my mother by his side. She had his head on her lap. Blood was oozing out of his temple. She kept wiping the blood but it would keep coming out. Maybe, she thought

he had fallen down, because she couldn't believe someone would shoot him', Praveen recalls.

'Father's last rites were done seven days later, on the 17th. It happened in Ghaiziabad in a hall kind of a place. Very basic. Not sure who gave the money for that. We were all crying all the time.'

'Everyone was sad. My new brother-in-law was very supportive. He is a very nice person, always helped us out.'

'LK Advani was the first political figure to reach out to us' Vimla says.

'After the incident, we were all supposed to be in the house itself. Not going anywhere until the police had completed their investigations. So, for 36 days we were all kind of under a house arrest, not allowed to leave town.'

'But before that, we got a letter from Canada in which Khalistanis had claimed they were responsible for the murder of DS Tyagi', she adds.

'My brother would keep me sedated for most parts because the incident became very traumatic for me.'

'Police caught the man who had gone to buy milk. They suspected him, followed him and caught him inside the house. He had a diary. Sheila Kaul was urban development minister then. Her name was also there in the diary, along with Tyagi's name.'

'Even when the terrorists had started the surveillance a month or so ago, when I started getting suspicious, I would tell him there's someone watching us from the window, there is someone here, there, he was so lost in his own perfect world. Devendra would ignore any such anomaly and would just walk straight past such things. Indifferent to the outrageous world. Lost in his books, his work, his friends', Vimla laments.

'On the day of his death ... he asked me not to come early', recalls VN Mishra, Devendra's friend and colleague.

'He said... what's the need, what will you do coming early? Do your morning prayers and come by 11-12, at your own time.'

'Otherwise, I would also have been there in the morning to witness the unfortunate incident. He even told my wife to not let me come early, to come *aaram se*.'

'I got a telephone call around 9 am from RP Sinha's house, he was the Director then. His wife was on the phone, told me that Sinha sahib has gone to AIIMS, you also go there asap, he's calling you.'

'At the time, I thought my son, who had left early for an exam, must have got injured somehow and which is why Sinha has gone to see him, and is also asking me to come fast.'

'I immediately stopped my prayers and got dressed, and first went to Sinha's house who lived only a few blocks from my place. There, Mrs Sinha tells me that it's Tyagi, that someone shot him.'

'Then I went to AIIMS, and I saw Sinha there. He informed me of what had happened, that he

was shot at in his home and was brought here dead; he was shot dead. Sinha told me, Tyagi's body is still in the hospital…if I wanted to see.'

'I said, what will I do seeing his body? I called up my wife and told her what had happened and she came straight to the hospital. She came and directly went into the emergency room where the body was kept, and asked them to show him to her. When they said who are you, she said see, he's my brother-in-law, show him to me right away!'

'Delhi was on red alert, vehicles had begun to be checked by that time.'

Times had changed. The city had changed. The country changed after that. Of course, the government compensated the victim family with a petrol pump and agency for selling fuel oils. Vimla says, her employees cheated her, knowing how naïve she was in worldly matters. No one was really kind and considerate to her.

The investigation into DS Tyagi's killing proceeded at snail's pace. Naturally, it was easy to blame unknown Khalistanis, that's what the police did. But they could never provide the family conclusive evidence that a political grouping was involved. They could not present any proofs to satisfy the courts. In Delhi's recent history, DS Tyagi's killing remains a question mark.

'I was brushed aside so often by everyone. Even after Devendra's death, when so many important people kept visiting the house to offer their

condolence, I was not allowed to see or meet anyone. My brothers and his brothers would rush to see those ministers – Shatrughan Sinha, LK Advani… they would not let me meet them', Vimla says.

As an elder brother Dr Umesh Tyagi describes Vimla's struggle post Devendra's assassination as not only 'inspiring' but he also highlights how his sister struggled for the survival of her family and also succeeded in recovering her life and excelling in her endeavour gradually, without seeking anybody's help.

He also likened his sister's courage with that of Helen Keller, where she fought against all the odds at a stage when her daughter's wedding was all set to happen. The way Vimla carried herself in the aftermath of her husband's death has been not only a learning experience for the younger generation but also for hers elders.

Vimla's parents were no more, and her natal household had dispersed, all the brothers and sisters married and leading their own lives. Her daughter Prerna and son Prashant too chalked out their careers and lives abroad. Vimla lived in India's capital city with her youngest son, grappling with the reality of life without Devendra, continuing to wonder 'why'?

'I had a good run till the time my luck lasted, and then I hit a red light, and it was such a sudden and violent stop at that red light', Vimla concludes.

Vimla Tyagi's husband Devendra Singh Tyagi
Chairman of the Commission for Agricultural Costs and Pricing, 1992